T0064265

Who Am I?
What Am I?
Why Am I here?

**Be curious,
not judgmental**

Who Am I?
What Am I?
Why Am I here?

A DISCUSSION ABOUT THE PERCEPTION OF REALITY

geoffrey barraclough

(my *experience* as...)

PARTRIDGE
A Penguin Random House Company

To order additional copies of this book, contact
Toll Free 800 101 2657 (Singapore)
Toll Free 1 800 81 7340 (Malaysia)
orders.singapore@partridgepublishing.com

www.partridgepublishing.com/singapore

I AM WHO I AM because of who we ALL are

Dedicated to

There is only one person to dedicate this book to
the often derided,
the often laughed at,
the often dismissed as a crank,
but ultimately the *chosen* man of history,
a *true* genius and free-thinker ...
Mr. David Icke
(or rather his 'experience' as)
Who started my journey to enlightenment,
...to remembering
'Remember Who You Are'
(the title of one of David Icke's books)
Well David – I remembered!
Thank you...

Honorary mentions to
micheal of the tellinger family
who is the most likely man on the planet to end
the ruling cabal's strangle hold on our false reality.
And

Mr. Mike King
of the 'Anti-New York Times'
and Tomatobubble.com
whose perceptive and incisive
insights enable him to see through 'The Globalist's'
propaganda and machinations like transparent glass.
And

LeeCaroll/Kyron
the possessor of probably the
most hypnotic mesmerising, and
inspiring voice on the planet.

Who am I? What am I? Why am I here?

Geoffrey Barraclough is the name I was given when my Soul/Spirit/Consciousness (whatever you would you like to call it) was reincarnated this time around.

I am *not* Geoffrey Barraclough – this is merely a corporate name I was endowed with to ensure I became the property of the Corporation of the United Kingdom and a controlled and programmed wage-slave for the world controlling Royal bloodline and Jewish Cabal.

I am merely having an ''experience' in this current dense 3D world, that we call reality as

Geoffrey Barraclough.

I am (jointly) responsible for the rebirth of two beautiful Souls (I call my daughters) and who are also learning (and remembering) knowledge from their current 'experience of life'

I was born (reborn) in England in 1953.

In my current 'life experience' I am a teacher

(of Art and Design) and I currently live in Vietnam.

I was 'awakened' in early 2012.

Contents

All our
Knowledge
has its
origins
in our
perception

Leonard da Vinci

Foreword

Because this thesis is written with love and pure intent, it is perhaps only fair that I give you a *warning* - reading this <u>WILL</u> change your life. Perhaps only a little, possibly quite significantly and maybe even *TOTALLY...!*

Consider carefully before you continue, you cannot un-read my noesis contained within, nor can you un-know the knowledge you will find here. To say there are *challenges ahead* to your 'belief system' is a gross understatement, and if your current beliefs about life are entrenched and dogmatic, and you want them to remain that way, I would advise you to stop reading right now and go and watch TV. I will take no offense if this work remains unread and if you are holding a 'hard' copy you can always use the paper as emergency toilet tissue!

On the other hand if you continually shy away from all, or any, contentious postulations you will forever remain (perhaps happily?) with your very restricted range of knowledge and limited left-brained (half-brained) mind-set.

The choice, as they say, is yours...

To understand yourself; is that a discovery or a creation?

Read further at your own risk...

Preface

My brother, when confronted with any new information (knowledge) that I may pass on to him regarding the 'Reality' of life will accept it with an open mind and mild curiosity. He is not prone (very often) to a knee-jerk outright dismissal reaction, even when presented with the most 'challenging' (to his belief system) of subject matter. However his normal response is something like - "Well that's all well and good, but what can I do about it? How does that affect me? Why should I want to know that?" In my experience the great majority of people, who are able to, at least *accept* new concepts of what life and reality really is, react with a similar point of view. "Huh, great, so what?"

In this book I am going to be revealing some very incitive and challenging but very true and *real* knowledge which, unless 'life' has already ground you down to zombie-like disinterest in everything, other than your own mind-set, *will* cause you a reaction of some kind. Incredulity, rolling your eyes, outright denial, scepticism, curiosity, pause for thought, argument, consider the possibly, acceptance, perhaps even agreement. But, in the end you will also probably think as my brother does..."hmm yes, very interesting...when does Coronation Street start, or what time is the football on?" This would be a shame (for you and *everyone* else) if you feel this way - a missed opportunity to become more enlightened, increase the collective vibrations of the planet, and be more in-tune with creation, but life, as you 'believe' it to be, goes on either way.

During the early days of my 'awakening' (which is the acceptance and understanding that life is totally *not* what it seems) I also felt this way. I just knew in my heart, inwardly, innately, that most of the information I was assessing *was* true, but in the beginning I thought - so what, how did having all this new knowledge really effect my life? The answer is – eventually it did, in so many profound ways. Totally changing my life-style and studying the equivalent of a Ph.D. and writing this publication are not the least of them. As I will explain later, accepting the knowledge I present here – or not, *will* have a significant influence on the quality of your life, and the lives of your children and grandchildren (if applicable) in the future. A lot of the knowledge here, regardless of its contention, is really quite self-evident, if you care to open your eyes and your mind to see it.

Each individual person on this planet *is, w*as created to be, individual, but at the same time we are *all* a part of one collective 'Consciousness'. David Icke succinctly illustrated this point...imagine each person on Earth to be a wave in the Ocean. Each wave is similar, but of course different, individual, but *all* the waves are an equal part of the Ocean. And this is how the World is, *everything*, including Earth itself, is an equally important and vital part of a collective consciousness. You may think right now that you are just a tiny insignificant speck in the greater whole of time and space and existence. I am only me, I have no influence on world affairs – or even on local affairs. I am just a person going about my business trying to survive through life the best I can. Well, if you think that, you couldn't be more wrong. You are (whoever you are) just as significant and important to this planet, Universe and the whole of Creation, as everyone else. The *only* reason you think you are only 'just little me', 'nobody special', is because, through 'programming', you have learned to give your power away and impart it onto someone else - your parents, your teachers, the police, the politicians, the president, the Queen, the King, anyone, who you *think* is your 'superior'. There is NO ONE on this planet who has any more right to be here than you. There is NO BODY on Earth who is your 'superior' (nor inferior) in any way. What you do and say and think has a much greater effect on *everything* than you can possibly realise, especially if you are coming from the perspective of - I am only 'little me' in a great big World.

Every experience you have, every piece of knowledge you accumulate throughout your life is added to the 'Ocean', to the collective consciousness of existence, and is just as vital as anyone else's. Wow, fine words, very motivating, but it just sounds like a lot of 'New Age' baloney to me. I hope, during the forth-coming pages, that I can impart to you sufficient knowledge, with evidence, to convince you that these 'fine words' are nothing more than a simple statement of fact.

Knowledge

Common knowledge (information) comes from money... if you seriously think about it for a moment there really can be *no* plausible argument against this! *Somebody* pays the historians and scientists and reporters to write about events and outcomes and, of course, that *somebody* wants only the 'knowledge' that 'they' have paid for.

Is there anything that money <u>cannot</u> buy? ONLY *one* thing...*UNCONDITIONAL* LOVE. There is *NOTHING* else (enough) money cannot buy...Money has the power to buy anything...even knowledge...*especially* knowledge!

It is said that the 'winners' always write history...and that's true in the sense that it's the people who *control* the *money* who are *always* the 'winners' and they write the version of history that suits them, in pursuit of their agenda.

Concerning knowledge there is one fundamental thing you must be aware of, the World *is* ruled, controlled and manipulated by an "Elite" group of *mega* rich Zionist Jews and 'Royal' bloodline families. These people are so rich that they can buy and acquire *anything* they want, and they have. They *own* or control all the major corporations in the world – Oil (energy,) Pharmaceutical, Food production, Banking, Media (TV, newspapers,) Entertainment (Hollywood) – they also control most of the governments in the world - and the Education systems...including ALL the major sciences and medical teaching and research facilities. They *own* knowledge. They manipulate and create – and ensure that 'their' version of knowledge is written and recorded.

What is Knowledge?

Knowledge, regardless of the source of it, is simply *What You Believe.* So the real question is not what is knowledge but - *What* do you believe, and why? For example I believe (based on research and connecting different information – and empirical evidence.) that there are many races of ETs interacting with people on planet Earth right now! So that is my *knowledge*. How many people would disagree with me? Of course if you disagree your knowledge is different from my knowledge - based *only* on your belief system, as opposed to my belief system.

Has *TRUTH* got anything to do with knowledge...the short answer is *NO!*

There is, in fact, very little *truth* in any of what we would consider 'common knowledge'. Does this matter though? If 'common knowledge' is believed by most people is it important if it is actually true or not?

For example...most people *believe* (knowledge?)

* that governments are elected to serve the people
* the problems with the economy are due simply to the natural cycles of business...
* the destruction of the Twin Towers on 9/11 was a Muslim Terrorist plot...
* the education system is designed to improve the minds of young people...
* the 'Holocaust' was the evil gassing of millions of Jews...
* global warming (Climate Change) is a result of man-made pollutants...
* cancer is a deadly and virtually incurable disease...
* the televised Moon Landings were one of mankind's greatest achievements...
* man evolved from lower life forms...
* modern medicine increases health...
* human interaction with Extra Terrestrials is science fiction...

How would you feel if I told you ALL this 'common knowledge', that you might believe, is <u>not</u> based on facts! There is actually *NO* truth in any of this 'knowledge'. Is this just my opinion? How do I 'justify' portraying this information as being untruthful and false knowledge and not just my personal opinion? I have used *independent* science research (not bought-and-paid-for mainstream science) evidence, emotion and intuition, reason and faith, and human sciences (connection to higher consciousness, psychic, 'channelling', innate knowledge and instinct) as ways of knowing, and also *critical thinking*. With an open-mind and a little independent research in the right places and some thoughtful consideration a lot of *real* knowledge actually becomes quite self-evident.

If anyone continually disbelieves everything that does not come from the 'mainstream' – what they are really saying is…

"It's no good telling me that, my mind is already made up - based on what I have been told to think by (mainstream) doctors, scientists, teachers and news programs.…so please don't confuse me with the TRUTH!" John Hamer…researcher/ author

So how do you ever know what the *real* truth is – if you are given different versions of the same 'knowledge' by different people? Research for yourself - not only in the (highly controlled, edited and often deliberately manipulated) mainstream, but also alternative viewpoints. It is very unwise and intellectually foolish, to dismiss out of hand any information (knowledge) you come across that your own belief system simply does not allow you to accept, without first serious consideration, reflection and critical thinking about it. Of course, by the same token I do not suggest that you believe everything – or even anything, that I have written in this book, without question. However, unless you can approach reading this – or anything, with a genuinely open mind, you will be forever trapped and controlled by your 'programmed' belief system, and all your knowledge will always be based solely upon mainstream 'programmed' group-think, and will have no relation what-so-ever to the truth.

...and the truth shall set you free...

We don't see things as they are,
we see things as we are...

Introduction

Who am I? – What am I? – Why am I here?

There cannot be many mature people on this planet who have not asked themselves these philosophical questions – or, at least fleetingly considered them at some point in their lives. They are the fundamental cogitations to the whole purpose and reason of being - of Human life on planet Earth.

Who am I?

I am a male person with a distinctive personality and characteristics.

What am I?

I am a Human Being.

Why am I here?

To struggle through life as best I can.

Ah, easy questions to respond to with simple answers, but, of course, there is so much more to it than that. In exploring these questions I will be principally doing so from a personal perspective – however overall, I will be explicating in all inclusive terms what it is to be *human* Humans (there are other types of Humans on Earth) and who *we* are, and what *we* are, and why *we* are here.

Of course this profound subject matter is hugely complex and the questions challenging to answer and to adequately explain in a relatively short dissertation. It cannot be done in an easy and flowing start-at-the-beginning, finish-at-the-end way. There are so many diverse and complicated concepts and constructs that each need to be appreciated before any attempt can be made to bring the whole thing together in a compendious and credible manner. So this book will consist of many different sections with each one explaining certain succinct aspects of 'reality' that are each vital to the reasoning of my contentions. They are not in any particular order, the order of each section is not a concern, and they may seem totally random, however each section develops queries that are addressed in another. Please bear with me in this, as when completed, all the subdivisions will add up to an understandable conception, even if to you, an unendurable one.

The hardest part about listening is to not fill in the gaps with your perceptions but to clear the mind and be willing to understand something new.

1
How do I Know?

If, as I have stated, most people in the world have considered the enigma of who and what we are and why we are here, then there must be some far more clever and intelligent people than me (not superior note, just more 'learned' in some areas) scientists, physicists, astrologers, biologists, philosophers and all manner of experts, who have studied these questions in detail. So, who am I to posit the answers to these highly scholarly questions? I am simply someone who has approached this monolithic and contentious subject with a *totally open mind* - not hindered by a programmed belief system, nor the need to conform and accept whatever I am told, or being biased towards any viewpoint by dogma, or having to support one theory over another at the cost of losing my job. This (unfortunately) makes me somewhat unique among serious enquirers into this area of Human existence. Also I am equipped with a seemingly precocious innate knowledge and understanding of how all the different and diverse connexions connect together to intelligibly form the axiomatic answers to these questions.

There are also many highly intelligent people, and other entities, in the world who *do* know – with absolute certainty who we are, what we are and why we are here, and I have studied and weighed the hypothesis' of many of these people during my research. I have seen incontrovertible evidence in many cases which prove my initial understandings, and some very compelling evidence in other cases which has given me the confidence of knowing I'm on the right track. Modern private science (as opposed to the heavily controlled and suppressed *mainstream* sciences) has also weighed in with some significant discoveries that substantiate many of my assertions.

Does anyone *really* believe that 'life, today with the endless wars and senseless death, the interminable and evil exploitation of people, the corruption, pollution, waste, poverty and famine, disease and the pointless and reckless destruction of nature, was how our beautiful and perfect planet was destined to be?...Come on, what 'Creator' - or God, if you like, would design a planet, a home, as perfect as Earth just for all the 'shit' that is happening on it? No way was it supposed to be like this! So, this sorry state of affairs would suggest that something serious went wrong somewhere along the line. And that is exactly what happened.

To write the complete background, to enable me to adequately and convincingly explain incisively what went wrong with our exquisite planet and why, would take, at least a 900 page volume. A man, with far more knowledge and experience than me, has already written it. It is called "**The Perception Deception**". Inexhaustibly researched and written by the world renowned researcher and author David Icke. I am not being sycophantic when I suggest that he is one of the greatest men (if not *the* greatest man) in history at enlightening, exposing and teaching the *real* truth of reality.

I absolutely recommend (in fact it is *essential* to read) this book. Meanwhile let me precis the things that went awry on our planet and why, in considerably less than 900 pages.

People are blind to reality and see only what they want to see....

2

Challenging Belief Systems

The answers to the questions about the reasons for our existence on Earth are, of course, complex and challenging to comprehend without a Brobdingnagian degree of open-mindedness and an acceptance of all possibilities; including some that will totally obliterate most people's belief systems. 'Nah, don't believe that mate you're crazy', is the usual (tedious) response to hearing anything that is antithetical to the accepted norm. Of course this knee-jerk reaction is based on ignorance, nothing more, and is really just a way of expressing an opinion based on delusion without any consideration, or research or real interest. A glib and easy response that protects a person's (misguided) beliefs in religion, or evolution, or in their own (very limited) conceptuality of what is real.

There is a vast amount of books written (including the Bible and the Urantia Book - *purported to have been codified by extra-terrestrial entities*) that each go some way towards connecting the multiplex of connections that make up the answers to the many questions about Human life. I have researched and studied many of these books and also a vast number of the informational videos by independent researchers posted on Youtube. The result of my personal conclusions, drawn from all the information I have accumulated over many thousands of hours of study, and my own innate 'knowing' is presented here.

Call me crazy, a dumb tin-foil-hat conspiracy theorist, or easily deluded thinker, or a sap-head, whatever, but before you show your own ignorance by doing so, consider this locution; Knowledge is gained by acknowledging what we don't know – Ignorance is shown by verbalising it. To simply deny, repudiate or disbelieve this information out-of-hand, may help to protect your ingrained, imposed and intractable belief system, but without your own thorough and informed research and contentions to oppose my findings, you are surely in a most tenuous position intellectually to utter any negative or dismissive comments.

What creates a rigid 'belief system' in the first place? A narrow perception of what is real, due to the restriction of the (very limited) five senses we have to interact with the world. The teacher teaches the teacher and obviously if the first teacher is wrong – or perhaps I should say not correct, then all subsequent teachers will be incorrect. Parents, through no fault of their own, bring up their child in the way they know, in a way they were taught by their parents and when the child grows up and becomes a parent, of course allowing for modern updates, the same process carries on. The school education system, at the teacher level, continues to unintentionally misinform and reinforce false notions, due to the counterfeit knowledge the teachers received. (This intention however is quite deliberate by the *controllers* of the educational system). This misinformation is continued at University level and by then a dense 3D limited view of life becomes totally ingrained and extremely difficult to abjure.

Think about it, a person has spent twenty years of education, much of it required hard work and study and sacrifice of time and social enjoyment to learn and become 'qualified'. That person (you?) does not want to agnise that it was really all for nothing, in terms of *true* knowledge. The knowledge they have 'learned' is now their own and very difficult to give up.

Here is Mike King's (tomatobubble.com) take on the education system...

During the formative years, children are praised for parroting back their ABC's and 123's. At an early age, the child's delicate mind is already being conditioned to equate obedient regurgitation with praise, love, and self-worth.

The brightest young 'learners' (memorisers) are singled out to receive the most praise. Proud parents enthusiastically reinforce the praise of the teacher, showering the impressionable child with hugs and kisses. The inflation of the 'intelligent' child's ego, and the reflexive association of 'regurgitation' with rewards, (including parental love!) are taking root. With subjects such as reading, writing, and mathematics, the system of obedient regurgitation and praise is a necessary and effective model of teaching. That's because the '3 R's' are what they are. They cannot be distorted. But with subjects such as History, Humanities, Economics, and the Sciences, the regurgitation/ reward model leaves the student vulnerable to manipulation and erroneous information[*]

The ego-gratification associated with the regurgitation & praise model is reinforced throughout Middle and Secondary School. It is during this time that the, 'gifted & talented'

---

[*] *(usually given unintentionally – a teacher has taught the teacher)*

students (who can regurgitate the most) are separated out from their 'inferiors' and taught to believe and repeat such rubbish as:

The Civil War was about slavery (It wasn't)

Germany started 2 World Wars (They certainly didn't)

6 Million Jews were gassed in 'The Holocaust' (A hoax))

Picasso was the greatest artist (He was more an opportunist)

Einstein was the smartest man on Earth (haha)

Martin Luther King was a Saint. (Quite the opposite, in fact)

Capitalism is about greed. (Read the section about greed)

Socialism is about charity. (Socialism is the same as fascism)

Men and women are the same. (Oh, really..?)

There is no such thing as race. (Eh?)

Man 'evolved' from pond scum (Yeah right!)

Global Warming is a fact. (It is a contemptible and pathetic hoax)

There are no government conspiracies. (There are NO true governments)

The next big 'doggie-treat' for the young 'straight A' 'parrot', comes when he – or she, is accepted to a 'prestigious' University. Now he knows that he is really smart!

At college/university, the 'star' student continues (for further reward and credit) to regurgitate ever more complex (but counterfeit) material that he is introduced to. Because he never learned to question the veracity of the school taught content he was exposed to, why would he question anything else he is taught at University, or might find in a text book or 'official' publication?

By now, the bright young scholar has been so psychologically conditioned that he is incapable of distinguishing between any fact-based regurgitation and propaganda/misinformed based regurgitation. His ego is literally addicted to the praise and good grades of whatever godlike (but misguided) Professor is instructing him. The hard-earned (and expensive!) diploma/ degree represents the ultimate 'doggie treat' and confirmation, in his mind, that he now knows it all.

Whenever challenged on his belief system, the 'educated' citizen's entire self-worth is suddenly threatened. Telling him for example that Global Warming (Climate Change) is a bunch of Marxist hooey is the equivalent, in his reactive mind, of saying that 2 + 2 is not 4! Because his bloated ego simply cannot bear the discomfort of being out-of-sync with the 'in-crowd', this (mis)educated person will despise you, and insult you for telling them anything other than what they want to hear...

This is not an exact verbatim extract...the actual article that Mike King wrote is heavily Americanised and I have made some slight alterations to it to make it more accessible to International readers. The full, unabridged, article can be found here - http://www.tomatobubble.com/libtards.html

This totally confirms my own view of the *deliberately* defective (virtually world-wide) educational system. It was purposely designed to give a false impression of life and the history of mankind, to cover up the real truth about reality. Education, as it is today, is not much more than a distraction to keep children away from finding out how much power and true-worth they each have as a Human Being, and how much influence each can really have on the world in which they live (more about this later). The controllers (of the world) cannot allow any *real* education to take place, otherwise their control would, of course, be over.

I will say as a teacher myself (fortunately I teach Art and Design - a right-brain subject and I am not a part of the disinformation process) that teachers and most educational professionals genuinely believe in the education system, they fervently believe in what they are doing and they work in, what they perceive to be, the best interests of the students. And, of course, there *are* many positive aspects to (any) 'education' in the development of a Human Being. But I long for the day when *real* and meaningful 'education' (spiritual, organic, ecological, supernatural, worldly, loving and *truthful*,) takes place universally, instead of just on the isolated and relatively few (but now ever expending in number) Online websites and Youtube presentations and (hard to find, under advertised) alternative publications.

The surest way to corrupt a youth is to instruct him to hold in higher esteem those who think alike than those who think differently.

3

Those 'Crazy Conspiracy Theorists'

Let me ask you a couple of questions here; Do you think that so-called "conspiracy theorists" that most 'sheeple' (people who are conditioned throughout their lives towards group-think and who eventually succumb to *only* accepting the mainstream 'norm') decry and deride as cranks and crazies, are just 'lucky' when their, so-thought, 'ridiculous' claims actually come to pass? People, such as 'crazy-man' (the UK Queen is a Reptilian-Alien) David Icke or Lee Carroll ('channeller' for a multidimensional higher Being known as Kryon) or founder of Exopolitics (the serious study of Extra Terrestrial relations and politics in the Omniverse) Alfred Lemont Webre, are they really just merely deluded, brain-sick lunatics, worthy of nothing more than derision? The problem with this belief is that time and time again *everything* these people have been saying and predicting, for well over 20 years now, has actually happened! Unfortunately for the deriders (and so-called debunkers) and their ill-conceived and subsequently pampered belief systems, the *truth* becomes a far too bitter pill to swallow. And so they write vitriolic comments about them, and often (senseless) insults, wherever they can. And these comments usually have the desired effect – to reinforce group-think, to persuade people that, despite the clearly obvious truths being revealed, it is still safer to maintain the accepted (but delusional) 'authority' point of view and to simply dismiss, without consideration or thought, any other knowledge.

Again unfortunately for people with ego-driven, dogmatic beliefs, if something is predicted or suggested by those who they simply write off as *crazy* 'conspiracy theorists' actually happens and manifests (as it always does) it (surely?) diminishes the credibility and, the self-deluded, intellect of these automatic, habitual, non-critical thinking, nay-sayers. There are also people (known as 'trolls') who are paid or persuaded to post malicious and derogatory comments on the websites and Youtube channels of these "Reality Truth Seekers" – shall we call them, to attempt to sway, the easily manipulated, public's opinion against all possibility that there might be some real and factual knowledge being offered. And then, of course there are the simple dim-witted morons who offer nothing more than infantile insults in response to anything that is not in their (very) limited view of reality.

Now ask yourself a question; Why aren't people with, shall we say, 'alternate' views ever invited on (or if they *are* – it's very rarely) to mainstream media for their interpretations of 'reality' to be exposed to the public on an equal basis with those of the 'establishments'? Of course the answer is that the views of the (disparagingly-called) 'conspiracy theorists' are *known* to be the most valid ones by the controllers and pay-masters of the mainstream media. There is no way they can be allowed to be heard...I mean, come on, if you controlled something for your own benefit would you allow anyone to start telling the people you control, that they are really 'omnipotent' Beings with a powerful mind of their own, and an ability to have incredible influence on their world? Of course not!

Personally I am happy to be, even if disparagingly, called a 'conspiracy theorist' - indeed I consider myself to be one. However this term is not correct I, and others like me, are in fact 'conspiracy *detectors*' and there is an ever increasing number of 'us'. If I am deemed, by most people, to be worthy of only rolled eyes and sympathetic looks towards the heavens, I don't care, I am in good company with some of the world's greatest, *open-minded,* critical thinkers, thank you. I am also a part of a quickly and exponentially growing group of the population who have had the 'veil' lifted and who are daily improving the quality of their lives as a result. Whenever I talk to people and express my knowledge, which is not often when in the company of obviously left-brained, dogmatic (non) thinkers, and I get the usual and highly predictable rolled eyes and 'sympathetic' smile in response to what I am saying, I simply tell these people to remember what I have just said and try to recall it in two or three years' time. I know unequivocally that I will have the last laugh as more and more people will inevitably 'awaken' and the current 'alternative' and much ridiculed and derided view of reality will become more and more widely accepted as the 'norm' - as it should be.

It is getting really exciting to see that the once rarely visited 'alternate' websites and Youtube presentations are now getting thousands, or even hundreds of thousands, of views nowadays, and there are so many more of them coming Online by the day. Sufficient proof in my mind of the mass 'awakening' of the world's population currently, and quickly, gaining ground - despite all the best efforts of the orthodox and (ill) 'educated' sceptics and debunkers, who think they know better, desperately throwing scorn at anyone who dares to be different.

I am often asked how reliable the information on the Internet is...well, the Internet is the biggest library and source of information (knowledge) on the planet. There is hardly anything that cannot be found Online, that is available anywhere else. Of course the Internet also makes it as easy to post and access disinformation as real information. So one has to be very careful when obtaining their knowledge from online websites. Let's take Wikipedia for example – this is supposedly the ultimate encyclopedia in the world and font of knowledge, and which is the first port of call for most people when doing research - for virtually any subject. However Wikipedia is a highly censored and controlled mainstream website, which has professional reviewers continually changing and editing, and in some cases deleting, information that is posted on it. Anything that does not conform to the 'establishment's point of view is altered or censored. Even worse, often deliberate dis-information, to hide real truths, is mixed in with the information given. As I will explain in more detail later, the world *is* controlled and run, in the background, by a very small minority of mega-wealthy Zionist Jews and bloodline Royal families, and these people, in order to keep their dominance over the population suppress a lot of knowledge that may be detrimental to their tight control of the 'accepted' perception of reality which they are desperate to maintain.

On the other hand a site like Youtube is more reliable. Youtube can be, and is, regularly censored (videos are deleted) but the actual content of the videos posted cannot be edited or altered in any way. Of course many videos may each give alternate and differing versions of the same knowledge, so one has to be discerning and use critical thinking when using this website. But you will often find that there is a majority of videos purporting roughly the same or similar knowledge and this would add weight to the reliability of the information contained therein.

Don't take things personally.
What other people say about you is
their reality not yours!

4

The Root of all Evil

"Life is just a struggle then you die" or similar popular phrases did not just come about without reason and for the great majority of people on Earth, life being a struggle does seem to be the case. Of course the word 'struggle' is relative – for some the struggle is to find water to drink, for others it is a struggle to earn enough money for the essentials of a basic lifestyle and for others the struggle is to afford a second home and luxury holidays. Regardless of the level in society that you find yourself in, struggle is a word that will be applicable to you at some time during your life. But, should life - living on this beautiful and bountiful planet, be a struggle for anyone, at any time? Of course not...so why is it? ...Money!

They say that money cannot buy happiness...if we are talking about happiness in its purest (spiritual) form, then that is true and happiness, in these terms (the expression of unconditional love) cannot be bought with any amount of money. But there is *nothing* else that money cannot buy including superficial happiness. 'Money is the root of all evil' is another often quoted phrase, which has a high degree of verity to it. Money is actually nothing more than power. The more money a person has the more power they have.

Power is control and the more power a person has the more control (over others) they have. Money (power and control) in the wrong hands leads to corruption and dominance, which is exactly what has happened on this planet and is the origin of the above mentioned expression linking money to evil.

Imagine the world without money...Impossible – it couldn't work. Of course it could - it is how life was *meant* to be. Lose the money and the corruption and dominance cannot exist and the 'struggle' disappears. Money is not the result of the evolution of a trade and barter system, as most people believe, money is a deliberate invention designed solely for the purpose of power and control. Stop for a moment and do some basic critical thinking...money, and the work required to earn it, is simply a form of enslavement, and if you are enslaved a struggle is the inevitable result.

The preoccupation to earn 'a living', to earn money to live, is a worldwide occurrence. Without money a person cannot survive on this planet for long. Why should that be? Go on tell me...A planet as bounteous as Earth and its people need money to live here? Of course one can argue that in some exceptional circumstances, lost tribes in the Amazon etc. life here *is* possible without money, as it should be! But generally, in modern life money is the source of existence.

Please think about this - is the whole of the human race that dumb and stupid to simply get themselves into this position where money is an absolute necessity for life, by following the natural evolution of a barter system? Of course not. Money has always been used as a control system by the 'Elite' few who make it and own the most of it. From his or her first steps a person is being trained to earn money and then to give most of this money away (in taxes and debt interest) to the very people who already have the most of it. All through childhood and into adulthood *all* education, at whatever level – nursery to University, home-schooling, even the school of 'hard knocks' (no formal schooling) is simply geared to you getting a job, or whatever else it takes, to earn money. Then you spend the rest of your life on Earth as a slave to money, this cause of all evil. Surely there has to be more to human life than that. The problem is you (?) and nearly everyone else on the planet, simply thinks this is the 'natural' way of things, dog-eat-dog, survival of the fittest and dam the rest in the chase for (ever devaluing) money.

What actually can money buy? Of course the essentials for existence, food and water, clothes and shelter and an appropriate lifestyle, but after that it really is just a case of you can go farther than my far, and drive faster than my car, and look back at me from where you are...(hmm, the lyrics of a song?) but really that's it. Money can (often does) make someone feel superior to someone else with less of it, but does wearing a $2000.00 suit really make anyone any better than the person wearing a $50.00 suit, or even a boiler suit? Ah, but money is the substantive reward of hard work – the proof of someone's labour, inventiveness, creation or entrepreneurial skills, they deserve a bigger house and a faster car and more exotic holidays. Really? At the lower levels of society I guess this attitude has some validity, let's encourage little Johnny to work hard so that he can have a nice home to live in. But the higher up the ladder you go the murkier the waters become. I would suggest that there are very few genuine cases of proportionate rewards commensurate with *honest* endeavour. Misconduct, deception, corruption, and outright criminal activity are all too often the prerequisites to gaining a substantial fortune. The power of money is so frequently the root cause of the degeneration of the true nature of mankind.

Watch...

"All Wars Are Bankers Wars"
https://www.youtube.com/watch?v=p-0BPMwgKNA
for further information about the evil of money (power and control)

You will always define events in a manner
which will validate your agreement
with reality.

5

Greed

Is greed just a natural facet of human Human behaviour? It would certainly appear to be...but, no it isn't. So why is there so much greed in the world? We are *taught* greed from any early age, it is not a natural characteristic of a human Human Being. Greed is nothing more than a symptom of social status or an addiction. If there was no money in the world, and therefore nothing had any (monetary) value, there would be no status and so there would be no greed. For example: why does any person need jewelry? - A diamond necklace for instance – it serves no purpose at all except to show that the wearer has a lot of money to buy it with. Their place and 'status' as a person in society is (superficially) measured by how big and valuable the diamonds are. But, if there was no money in the world and therefore the diamonds had no value, and everyone could own a diamond necklace, after all diamonds are free in the earth, there would be no substantive need or reason to own one.

Money (and possessions) is simply an addiction to many people. Like a stamp collector, the more stamps a collector has, the more they want. A stamp collector with just a few stamps is unlikely to make it their sole purpose in life to obtain more, but a person with a bigger collection is much more likely to want to add more and more stamps to it. This is the same with money. The people with a lot of money are much more inclined to want more and more, than the people who have less money. Many people collect more money (cheat, steal and walk all over people to get it) than they could ever spend in normal circumstances and having this much money gives them feelings of great power, and perhaps achievement. I would suggest it is a pretty shallow life that relies on the collection of vast amounts of money as a sign of achievement. But whatever – everyone to his own I guess. Having lots of money is also said to give a person a sense of freedom and I can well understand that, that is one way of escaping 'enslavement'. But does the freedom of not having to work compare with the freedom of knowing, the freedom that true knowledge brings? That is for each individual to answer - and another question to answer is how did they 'collect' their money?

I would like you to consider conscience here. As I have just asserted, earning more than a 'comfortable' amount of money usually entails a lot more than just honest enterprise, and the suspension of personal integrity and conscience is often required to collect more than a just and fair amount of it. If you make, or create, or contribute towards, something of value, then, of course, you expect some form of fair remuneration for your efforts. If your natural or learned and developed skills are in demand – entrepreneurial, entertaining, teaching, healing, advising, book-keeping, judicial opinion, cooking, fire-fighting, farming etc. then you would expect an equitable reward for your time and degree of expertise. If your physical labour and hard work, building or cleaning for example, is required for the benefit of the community, then you would expect a fair wage for your time and effort. If you create a market for an honest and beneficial product and demand a *justifiable* price for it, good for you. But, if you cheat people, by fooling them into believing the skill, or thing, or product that you are supplying, is worth much more than would be considered as fair by knowing and experienced people, your conscience has to be over-ridden by your desire for money and, of course, this is a manifestation of cupidity brought on by money. And a great many people do fall foul of this avarice, this craving for the *power* money can provide. But this greed is simply a result of the altered and negatively affected human beingness, brought about and promoted by the fallacious concept of a status dominated society.

For example; is a Footballer, or Pop Star (or any person) worth $millions? Are the vast amounts of money being paid to sports stars or entertainers really proportionate with their value to a conventional, unhindered society? Of course not. Is the footballer being 'greedy' to negotiate a $multi-million contract for his (usually limited) skill-set that a team may require? No, he is simply reacting to an artificial value placed upon his ability to 'entertain' (distract) people by a highly manipulated society. The value of 'entertainers' was always a mystery to me, especially so-called sports stars. What is it that makes a person who has an ability to throw a ball through a hoop, or hit a small (golf) ball 300 meters, or who can run around a soccer field for ninety minutes, worth $millions? Why can a heavily armoured overweight guy who can charge into another heavily armoured guy on a football field, become a multimillionaire? A heart surgeon who saves lives every day, or a fireman who risks his life every day, or an organic farmer who works all hours to help feed people with real and nutritious food will never be multimillionaires. Yet who are really worth more to society? But, wait a moment...if you control society, the entertainers and sports stars are your most valuable assets (so pay them well) because they create interest and excitement and foster tribal (group-think) instincts and, above all, they distract people from all the problems in their lives...the very problems that you are creating on your way to further control. Greed is a creation it is not a natural state.

A person is regarded as being 'greedy' if they eat too much food, in comparison to someone else but, most food that is manufactured is deliberately designed to be addictive, designed to make you eat (and therefore buy) more of it - more profits for the manufacturers. But, without money there would be no cause for the food manufacturers to make food addictive just nutritious (oh, how I wish) and therefore there would be no greed. Greed is not natural. So the notion that if everything was free (no money needed) there would be many people who would want more than their share of everything, because they are naturally 'greedy', is simply not valid.

Life is not a problem to be solved, but a game be experienced

6

Everything is Free

Everything on Earth is free. Nothing is imported from another planet, everything a person could possibly need is already here - provided by nature. All the raw materials for *everything* can be found on, or under, the earth. These resources of nature should be, were meant to be, the fundamental birth-right of everyone born on this planet and without money (power and control) there would be no need to have to work to earn a living to afford them. Why do we have to pay for water? Water is plentiful and free, but it isn't free. Ah, we have to pay for the pipes and delivery systems into our homes... why? The pipes are free, made from the free raw materials provided by Mother Earth. Someone (the people with the most money - power and control) controls the supply of water for a *profit* – for money! Without money, and the power and control it buys, everyone on the planet would have more than enough water for all their needs without it being restricted to them by someone's imposed (for personal profit) cost.

We have to pay the people who work in the water industry (and the other industries that provide the products and services that we need). Why? If everything is free (as it should be) there is no need for anyone to have to earn any money to buy anything. Imagine the world without money.

You could go into a car dealership and order a Ferrari, for example, and have it delivered, any colour you want, without any thought of working overtime, scrimping and saving and going into debt to get it. In fact if you really wanted you could order three or four Ferrari cars because they are free. Made with free labour and from free raw materials, already here on Earth. Ah, that's just crazy, if they are free everyone in the world would want one and that's impossible. Well, everyone in the world would not want one and why would anyone want more than one? Without money a Ferrari has no value except as transport, it would not be considered as a status symbol as it is now. No one would look twice at you in a Ferrari, it is just a another form of transport, and with everything being free (including energy – including anti-gravity energy - *that already exists, but has been kept a secret*) there would be many, much more, efficient forms of transport to appeal to other people. Let's look a little further into this idea of no money in the world. If there is no money there would be no need to work, so who would actually make the Ferrari cars or the pipes for the delivery of water, or farm the food, or build houses, or make any of the things we need? OK, time for some more critical thinking here... Nobody would *have* to work for money, therefore could the task of making something, anything, really be considered as work? As we have already reasoned, money and working for it, is simply a form of enslavement. You will work or you will get no money and therefore you will not be able to buy anything, including essential food and water, so you have no choice, you *have* to work – consequently you are a slave. If you don't *have* to work then anything you do is by choice and so becomes a 'labour of love' and freewill.

Think of all the people in the world – all the different personality traits, all the different attitudes and interests they have, all the different abilities and capabilities they have. Think about the whole world being one giant community, and if that is too big a step for you, think about each country being a giant community, or each city, or each town, and everyone in that community is helping each other to make the very best of life. That would happen without money. There would be no need for competition – every man for himself (as is the case now). People would do work, not because they *have* to, but because they *want* to (a labour of love) to help the community and themselves enjoy their lives to an ever increasingly higher standard.

In the community there would be people who enjoyed gardening, for example, and they would be farmers or park-keepers, there would be people who enjoyed working with their hands, fresh air and keeping fit, and they would be the builders, there would be people who enjoyed science, and who enjoyed teaching, and who enjoyed fixing things and so on...They would do these jobs because they wanted to and everyone would benefit from them. But who would do the dirty jobs like cleaning the streets or working in the sewage industry? There would be many people who would want to do this, people who are unskilled, for whatever reasons, but they would be a part of a caring community and they would have pride in the community and their job would be recognised as being valuable and laudable. Just as important to the community as the scientist, or healer, or footballer. There would be no hierarchy of jobs without the social status of differential salaries.

Without the restriction of labour costs there would be no unemployment, every fit and able person could do a 'job' (labour of love), therefore there would be no need for anyone to 'work' eight or ten hours a day. The labours of love would be shared out among more people and consequently the 'working' day would be reduced, perhaps, to three or four hours. So you would 'work' at a job that you wanted to do for just a few hours a day and the rest of the time you could go to the beach, or go shopping to pick up, not buy, whatever you wanted. Ah, all this is airy fairy and is simply not possible. There is no possible impediment to this premise, it is actually what life and living was *meant to* be on this planet.

All the arguments about the 'lazy' people who would not do anything for the community, or the criminals who would just steal things, or the people who would try to take unfair advantage are groundless. If nothing had any (monetary) value and everything was free, why would anyone steal anything? Laziness is a conditioned malady, conditioned and labeled by a society that ostensibly overlooks anyone who does not seem to conform to the 'wage slave' orthodoxy. The 'lazy' people would willingly contribute to a community that would equally benefit them, and without money there is simply no cause for corruption or taking unfair advantage.

For a full and detailed description of life without money I highly recommend Michael Tellinger's fantastic and enlightened book **"Ubuntu Contributionism".**

How can one of us be happy if all the others are sad?

7

Empathy

I get really ticked off when, in a movie, the character sighs with despair and palms his face at all the destruction and death around him, or at the desperate state of poverty alongside extreme wealth, or at all the pollution and meanness in the world and he looks up to the heavens and plaintively blames human nature..."ah, when will *we* ever learn?"...etc. All these deplorable things are really nothing to do with real *human* human nature, they are the result of distorted and highly controlled human behaviour. These types of movies (as we shall see later) are merely, but quite deliberately, reinforcing a misguided notion that flawed human Human Beings are responsible for all the Mephistopheles of the world. This belief though is so far from the truth that, to me, it is just totally laughable and contemptible.

Empathy, the consideration of, and benignity to, others and caring about how they feel in consequence to our actions is the greatest and most natural attribute of the human Human Being - of *human*, human nature - not the selfish greed and thoughtlessness, and glib carelessness we are so often attributed with. *What....!?* Look at the world today...all the wars and destruction of human life, all the corruption, all the poverty and famine, all the dog-eat-dog competitiveness to get ahead (to earn more money) and all the every-man-for-himself mentality that pervades modern life. Where's the compassion and feelings for others there? The response to that inquiry is where we really start to explore the answers to the questions about who and what we are (it will become clearer soon). Enough to say here that we, human Humans are not what we are destined to be… yet! But never-the-less 'we' (collectively, the Human Race) are not the ones who are accountable for the wretched state of the world. I take no personal responsibility at all, nor should you, for the pollution, destruction, corruption and poverty, that is rife on Earth. It is out of our hands. Yes you can pick up your own litter and that would be great, but I am talking about the total absence of ethics and morality, and the astounding disdain for the environment and public health, which sees the dumping of industrial waste, in the air, on the land and in the rivers, on a massive global scale by all the corporations that are owned by the same people who are bringing in 'Agenda 21' on the back of 'man-made' pollution causing 'Global Warming'. (More about that later).

Given that empathy *is* probably the most naturally occurring and cardinal emotion of the human Human Being, there must be a reason and cause for empathy to be so manifestly absent in so many instances in this world. This overwhelming *lack* of empathy would suggest that someone, or something, more (or less?) than human, is deeply involved somewhere. This is the crux of the matter, indeed there are Alien 'entities' who *are* in tight control of the Human species and who are deviously distorting and perverting the natural humanness of us all for their own agenda. There is more, a *lot* more to human, human life on this planet than meets the eye. I keep using the term *human* Human Being as an adjective because there are Human Beings on Earth who are anything but 'human' (humane) in the accepted sense of the word.

"The secret of change is to focus all of your energy, not on fighting the old, but building on the new"

8
Evolution

Human life, in fact all 'life' on Planet Earth is alleged to be the result of a very slow and gradual evolution over billions of years. 'Life' was the happy accident of some primordial 'soup' consisting of just the right amount of chemicals and elements to spontaneously give rise to a single cell organism that eventually developed into a multiple-celled creature, that in turn developed into a more complex being, that eventually became a fish of sorts and from there into an amphibious animal...and so on. Really? Man had as much chance of being the development of a banana, than the result of the 'evolutionary process' involving a monkey. The whole theory of evolution, as proposed by Darwin is just that – a theory and a piteous one without any real (come on, even common sense) scientific basis or evidence, just lots of asinine conjecture and hypothesis' that have never been adequately (or even remotely) proved.

Why are there still apes on Earth if the natural order for things was for them to evolve into Human Beings? Where are the half-man half ape beings who are in the process of a presumably ongoing evolution? - or was evolution just a one-time deal, a once ever phenomenon? Why has evolution stopped? Oh, the conditions have to be just right for an ape to develop into a Human Being and nowadays the conditions are not right. Ah, that explains it…Heck, it's a good job that we had so much luck going for us in our development as a species then. *Everything* about Evolution it seems is just one happy accident after another. Come on, think about it – the complexity and miraculous combination of energy and biochemistry and spirit that is a Human Being has to be more than freakishly, unbelievably, fortuitous happenstance! Of course evolution within species has not stopped, but it would appear that Darwin's evolution of species into other species has just kind of petered out – maybe run out of luck…?

So, if life on Earth is not (as it *definitely* isn't) the result of the evolution fairy tale, where did life and, in particular human life, come from? God created life – it says so in the bible, in seven days, (huh?) The problem with this speculation is who or what is considered God? There are so many different deities purported to be God. The different 'Gods' of the great smorgasbord of religions certainly did not create man – these 'Gods' were, of course, the creations *of* man. These Gods are all the interpretations of – higher Beings/ aliens, or 'heavenly bodies' (the Sun and other planets), or mythical creatures.

Going back to the very beginning of 'life' *anywhere,* in any universe or in any dimension, there must have been some form of 'Creator' (call this Creator 'God' if you wish) – but let's call it what it is - the 'Source' (of everything) an 'energy', a Consciousness.

I understand that you may have deep-seated religious beliefs, taught to you at an early age and reinforced throughout your life by observance of fatuous ceremony and rituals, and I am sorry if I cause you offence. But perhaps it's time that you opened-your-eyes and take another, more considered, look at the mind-control that is Religion, the divide-and-rule cause of more suffering and death throughout history than all the diseases put together. The bizarre 'clubs and associations' (different religions) with all their different rules and regulations– and Gods, ruling over the masses by fear and constraint. I can understand the comfort and solace one might get worshipping a deity and believing in It (Him?) with all ones heart, pleading (praying) for assuagement or reward for living life as one should (?) but how really can there be *many* Gods (as all the different religious beliefs seem to propose) supposedly *all* be responsible for the creation and welfare of mankind? Do they all *share* the job between themselves?

Of course some aspects of religion can be benign and teaching 'Christian'/charitable behaviour to others is commendable, but "my religion is better than your religion" - which has been an all too pervading notion throughout history, is surely repugnant?

You are your *own* God. God is inside of you. God the Creator, the Energy, the Spirit – a benignant God, who will reflect your deeds and actions and thoughts back to you. No need for pleading (praying) just doing. You will get back from life whatever you want, if you genuinely work and live towards it. Praying in a Church, as earnestly as you can on bent knees, and then going out and continuing your life cheating and walking all over people to get ahead, to get more money, will get you nowhere, in a spiritual sense. Use some critical thinking here, instead of dogma and religious doctrine. The religious God is a human concept.

He (She?) is not a physical entity. So how can 'God' respond in physical terms to prayers and requests, how can God, other than in the imagination, grant anything? How can God interact, other than in the imagination, with mankind, in anything? How can God, other than in the imagination, be a threat to anyone? (Don't do that or God will punish you). The religious God is just another programmed belief system – a control system.

The true God, the Creator (of everything) is an *energy*, a consciousness, a supernatural force and as such, God can be whatever you want It (Him? - Her?) to be. God can be a creative force in your life, or equally a destructive one. God can be benign and forgiving, if you so wish, or God can be fearful and vengeful, if that's what you want to believe. God is not exclusive just to religions. God is in you, you are your own God, and with this mind-set you are, as you were meant to be, an omnipotent Being.

You are whoever you want to be...

9
How did Life on Earth Begin?

Some of the presupposed theory of how planet Earth was originally formed could have elements of truth in it, but personally I doubt it, based on my belief and understanding that nothing in creation is just random. But the *life* on Earth was unarguably *not* formed as postulated by Marxist, thirty three degree Freemason, 'New World Order' advocate and 'puppet' Charles Darwin and (bought and paid for) mainstream scientists. Life on Earth was 'seeded' by an advanced race of extra-terrestrial entities or Higher Beings. No way did all the different species of plants, insects and animals, and all the different races of Humans just happen to spring up by ergodic luck, from some lifeless 'primordial soup' - there is no stochasticity in nature. The planet Earth, when it was ready and suitable for sustaining life was seeded, like a garden. There is wide consensus among 'Interventionists' – people who believe that life was seeded by Alien entities – that there are just too many 'coincidences' and expedient happen-stance for the Evolution theory to be at all plausible. There are no coincidences in nature – *everything* is by design.

I heard recently of another highly dubious (mainstream science) theory about how life on Earth began, which basically involves a large piece of some, life supporting, planetary body breaking off and fortuitously crashing down on Earth. This fragment of rock (or whatever) then burst open and spread the seeds of all the life on Earth (haha). Why is it that science is so set on the life on Earth just being the result of a (billions and billions-to-one against) astrological chance event – or an incredible chemical fortuity? Of course the answer is – control. They, the controllers of the world and 'owners' (paymasters) of mainstream science, want you (need you) to believe that you are nothing more than a cosmic accident, or an implausibly lucky development of chemistry (from the same origin as a dung beetle) that you have no power yourself, you are deemed worthless, you are simply the result of chance. A belief system like that makes you so much easier to control and conform to your 'betters'!

And as far as 'God' being responsible for the beginning of all life, well, you have to choose which God, of the many candidates, it might have been, Although a nice story and the root of a safe and comforting belief system for many, like the chicken and the egg, you have to ask yourself which came first – God or man. Of course it was man who created the different (religious) Gods, not the other way around.

According to researcher Lloyd Pye, and many other serious and independent researchers, who I am in total accordance with, the conditions for any life to be sustainable on Earth *were*, started by single cell bacteria – but these bacteria called 'Prokaryotes' did not spontaneously arise naturally in the much vaunted 'primordial soup' they were introduced to Earth at exactly the time they were needed, when the young molten planet was cooling, in order to create the right conditions for the development of life forms.

There are two distinct types of Prokaryotes - which rather precludes the ideas of accidental spontaneity – and their job was to provide an abundance of oxygen and water vapour to our vernal planet. These organisms were totally indestructible and no amount of molten rock, fire, or harsh conditions, could stop their vital work in preparing the right atmosphere for life to begin.

Two billion years later, further, massively more complex single cell micro-organisms, 'suddenly' appeared on Earth called 'Eukaryotes'. These organisms took over from the Prokaryotes and further enhanced the conditions necessary for life. In a fantastic 'coincidence' (no coincidences in nature) the Eukaryotes appeared on Earth at *exactly* the right moment. Eukaryotes are not indestructible and they needed the right conditions (provided by the Prokaryotes) to survive and prosper. There is just no physical or scientific explanation for Eukaryotes to have simply appeared as a natural phenomenon. They arrived on Earth, were sent to Earth, not made on Earth – at *exactly* the right time, *not* accidentally, but as part of the seeding of Earth by Higher Beings.

What followed, over the next few billion years, once the atmosphere of planet Earth was made life sustainable by the introduction of the Prokaryotes, and then the Eukaryotes, was the development of a multitude of life forms. Plants and algae and creatures on the land and in the sea (which would have been fresh water at that time). Each of these life forms had distinctive DNA structures and different vibrational energy and were not (could not have been) all developments from the same single cell organism.

Although I have totally (and justifiably) decried and derided Darwin's imaginative evolution theory – I would concede and state that the gradual evolution of a species within a species does take place – this is called micro-evolution. However the evolution of one species into another different species (macro-evolution) reptile into mammal, ape into man, for example, as purported by Darwin, is simply preposterous. So this begs the question – how did all the different plants and creatures, that made up early life, suddenly appear and develop? This simply could not have been a natural, self-generated and unaided process. After thorough research and some serious critical thinking (and despite all the puerile theories of billions-to-one against lucky chances of cosmic, or chemical, accidents that mainstream science *want* you to believe) Intervention (deliberate seeding) becomes the *only* plausible explanation.

There is an accord among many researchers and people who are able to 'channel' information from Higher Beings, that a race of higher consciousness, extra-terrestrial beings called the 'Pleiadians' were responsible for the seeding and development of life on Earth – they were also responsible for the seeding of many other planets in the Universes. Of course there are also many counter-claims to this hypothesis that life was created on Earth by a race of Higher Beings – it could have been done by the 'Source'/'Creator' (Supernatural Intelligent Energy) of ALL life directly. But whatever the real truth is of who or what seeded Earth, (although highly interesting) is not critical to the advancement of this thesis. It is sufficient to know and appreciate that all mainstream counter-theories to life on Earth having begun with an off-world intervention by an alien hand of some kind, are severely and intellectually limited – to the point of being desperate.

For further information on this particular subject I would recommend reading "**Everything you Know is Wrong**" by Lloyd Pye – or viewing some of his many presentations featured on Youtube.

...And those who were seen dancing were thought to be insane by those who could not hear the music...

10

Nothing is Solid

By far the most fundamental thing to know and understand when pondering any questions about who we (Human Beings) are, is that there is no physicality, no solidity (as we understand it) in any of the universes or dimensions in existence. Basically everything...*everything*, is nothing more than a form of energy – vibrations /electrical wave forms. Ah, now that's just totally crazy – no solidity? If I stand in front of a moving car then some 'physical' damage, pain at the very least, will surely happen to me as a result of the solid car hitting me. I banged my head this morning on the shower door – it certainly felt solid to me and I even have a bruise to prove it was solid. OK, I grant you, this concept of nothing being solid is a hard one to comprehend. But on the other hand if all 'solid' things are made up of atoms (which they are) and an atom is ninety nine point whatever percent empty space (which it is) then how can 'solid' things be solid if they are made up of ninety nine point something percent empty space?

Everything in our life is simply a matter of perception. Think about it...we Human Beings have five senses; hearing, sight, smell, taste and touch. Now, how do these senses work? Well, sight is the result of light waves (energy) hitting the retina and then being decoded in the brain to reveal whatever object is being viewed, right? Hearing is the result of sound waves (energy) causing vibrations in the inner ear which are then sent as electrical impulses to be decoded by the brain as sound - talking, or music, or as the annoying barking of that dog! Smells are the same, electrical signals being decoded by the brain. Same with taste and of course touch. So, in actual fact everything 'solid' we see, feel, hear, taste and smell is simply the decoding of electrical signals (energy) received by the brain. Therefore our perceptions of the whole world are simply conceived in our head.

That's all well and good but explain the 'perception', if that is what it is, of being able to sit in an apparently 'solid' car and driving it from one place to another, or of sustaining a broken leg, or of death caused by (the perception of) a 'non-solid' (?) bullet. To adequately explain this is to go into the very core of what we Human Beings really are - patience we are getting there...

"Every one of the five senses can be twisted to deliver a completely different picture of the world. If by 'picture' we mean the sight, sound, smell, taste and texture of things, a troubling conclusion looms. Apart from the very unreliable 'picture' running inside the brain, we have no proof that reality is anything like what we see"

11

The 'Multiverse'

A Human Being is one of an incomprehensible amount of species or races of extra-terrestrial life that an unimaginable magnitude of universes and dimensions are teeming with. One German super computer simulation estimates that there are "500 Billion galaxies in our Universe" alone and astronomers now estimate there are 100 Billion habitable Earth-like planets in our 'Milky Way' galaxy and 50 Sextillion habitable Earth-like planets in our Universe. Physicists Andri Linde and Vitaly Vanchurin of Stanford University recently calculated..." that the total number of Universes in the "Multiverse" exceeds... 10 raised to the power (10 raised to 10 power 7) power 3

This is a number that cannot be written or fully comprehended - basically it is a 1 with so many zeros written after it, at 6 x zero's per inch, the number would stretch out to be 260 *million* miles long...!

The Dimensional Ecology of the Omniverse - Alfred Lambremont Webre

If each of these Universes also had 50 Sextillion habitable Earth-like planets in them - it's hardly likely that we humans we are the only life forms around..!

Oh come on, how can there be that amount of universes, our own known universe is totally humongous, beyond comprehension, so where's the room for trillions of trillions of trillions of other universes? - get real. Ah, remember everything, *everything* in existence is just energy. The hugeness of a universe is just a perception in the brain. OK if I accept that, where are all these supposed universes? We only ever see one. They exist outside of our (altered and distorted) Human Being ability to see them. Think of a TV – you press a button on the remote control and the channel on the TV changes. Has the first channel just disappeared from existence? No, of course not, you can press the button again and the original channel will return. How many channels can a TV receive? – theoretically an infinite number of channels (programs) can exist side-by-side, each on a slightly different frequency (energy). Well, the same principal applies to the endless number of universes and dimensions. Unfortunately, at the moment our (deliberately reduced and restricted) five senses do not enable us to 'switch over' to witness them. Hah, so if that's the case how does anyone really know they are there? Also you mentioned that our five senses have been intentionally damaged...by who, or what, and for what reason?

The answer to the first question, will also answer the second question. As I have declared previously the first fundamental thing to appreciate, before any comprehension of the nature of 'reality', and our place in it, can be understood, or even contemplated, is the credence that everything, *everything* in creation is a just form of energy – there is no 'physical'. Hah, but energy cannot be destroyed, only altered, so bang goes that theory - what happens when someone or something dies, is destroyed? Good question, but easy to answer. Nobody actually 'dies' as we understand death. Sure the body stops working due to trauma, disease or old age and eventually it rots away, but the biogenic 'energy', the Soul, if you like, of the person, or animal, or plant is sustained and 'lives' on (energy cannot be destroyed). A dead body does not rot away to nothing, it is changed to another form of energy – dust, or food for insects, or earth matter. A plant's energy, when it 'dies' is simply 'recycled' into another plant. The same precept applies to animals and humans. That brings us on to 'life' after 'death' and reincarnation, but more of that later, for now let's get back to the question about how does anyone really know that the whole multitude of universes really exist.

Another primal concept to accept, when dealing with the cognition of the true nature of reality, is that there *are* countless universes in existence and so, of course, there are an even greater amount of planets, a high percentage of which will be life (in some form) sustainable, and therefore, there are an equally unimaginable number of different living entities in existence. We are certainly *not* alone! How arrogant, or naive, of anyone who might believe we are! 'Many' (a totally inadequate word) of these other living entities are of a much more advanced 'intellect' (again a woefully inadequate word) than we Earthlings – some are even just manifestations of incredible consciousness (no apparent 'physical' bodies at all) and they *do* know about all the different universes and dimensions because they are capable of visiting and experiencing them, as *real* (enlightened) Human Beings will also be one day! There are some *extra-human* Humans who have sufficiently developed higher sensory powers to enable them to actually communicate with higher intelligent beings in a manner that is commonly referred to as 'channelling'. These people, if they are to be believed, have confirmed the existence of multiple universes and dimensions from information they have received from Higher Beings. Of course there are bound to be some charlatans who claim to be able to 'channel' information from advanced entities but are doing nothing except gaining attention to themselves, for whatever ego-driven reason, and these people give gleeful credence to the sceptics. But, equally there are also bound to be genuine 'channellers' who *can* and should be believed. Something to reiterate here is that *all* life, all existence, in *all* the universes and dimensions (*all* energy) has limitless potential. There are no limitations to what is possible on an incorporeal level, and this is my answer when I am asked 'how can we really know anything that's not obvious or visual'.

Imagine being of sufficient *intelligence* (inadequate word) to see, or experience, and understand with ease, the construct of a 'Multiverse' - to have or rather, to be able to use already existent extra sensory powers - above the very limiting five senses that dictate our current, very primitive, perception of reality. We would be 'super beings' capable of far more than 'struggling' with life in the lower dense 3D dimension of our current beingness. We could not be controlled by others' power and corruption (money). We would be free of all earthly (perceived) limitations and be able to live life as it was meant to be. So, that is the reason that our current five senses have been deliberately constricted. To enable us to be more easily controlled by power and corruption (money) by the entities who actually wield this control – more about this in a moment.

12
What Happened to us?

"Doctor Who", "Star Wars", "Star Trek" and many other Science 'fiction' movies and TV programs, have done a great disservice – as they were meant to do, to the general acceptance of Aliens on and visiting Earth. Most people (you?) immediately think of all the amazing and bizarre Alien creatures presented in these films and the, often, ridiculous make-up and comical mannerisms of the actors portraying the Aliens. When it is suggested to someone (you?) that Extra Terrestrial Beings are real this invokes laughter and derision and disbelief because, perversely, by being introduced to a multitude of different 'Aliens', they have been brain-washed into accepting that it is all just ludicrous science fantasy. But actually a great many (most) aspects of "Doctor Who" and "Star Wars" and "Star Trek" are based on *fact*. The writers and producers of these films 'are in the Know' - they *know* about the true nature of reality, as I am presenting it here, and they incorporate this knowledge into their productions, with the precise intention of making everything seem far too implausible to be true. 'Fact is often stranger than fiction' is a very true saying especially with regards to Aliens and space and time travel.

"Beam me up Scotty" is based on fact – the technology for this exists now and Extra Terrestrials (as already discussed) are fact. Time travel is more than a theory – indeed it is happening often, around the world at the present time. "Warp factor five" or whatever it is, is based on fact – the speed of light is not the fastest available speed to travel the Universe as often accepted, it is in fact, relatively slow. Mainstream physics *do not* apply except in the very limited and lowly 3D (three dimensional) perception of Earthlings. In higher dimensions *everything* is possible. Make a Google search 'exopolitics.com' for convincing explanations of all these phenomenon by whistle-blowers' and ex-military Black Ops personnel who have been part of the highly secretive on-going "Operation Phoenix" program in which time travel and 'jump room' travel to Mars and to other destinations have been developed and used. Apparently Barack Obama has participated in the Operation Phoenix program and has experienced travel, via a 'jump room' (teleportation) to Mars himself. Well, I can go and look, but there's no point because I still won't believe it – they must be insane cranks to say such things...this will be the likely response of those with entrenched, programmed, dogmatic and narrow-minded belief systems. But if viewed with an open and curious intellect there really is enough authentic and convincing testimony to sway even the most entrenched mind.

An interesting point to make here is that time does not actually exist – it is a conceptualisation created by Human Beings in the 3rd dimension. The past and present and future are all NOW! This is a very tricky construct to grasp, but think of it this way. Imagine a movie recorded onto a digital disc (DVD), the whole movie, everything that happens (it could be a film of your life) is contained on the disc 'now' in the present in your hand. You can play the disc and 'jump' to see what happens at the end of the movie, and you can 'jump' back to see the beginning, and, of course, anywhere in between, and everything you see is in the present 'now'. 'Near death' experiences (which I will discuss later) is where a person physically 'dies', for a period of time, and is later revived or makes a recovery. During this time the Soul/Spirit/Consciousness of the person leaves the body. Everyone who has undergone this process, always describes, among many other things, the seemingly time-less nature of the 'afterlife', all their experiences and memories seem to happen simultaneously in the 'now'.

Once you realise, and by now you are beginning to (surely?) that all we, as Humans, have is a tiny, infinitesimal range of frequency/vibrational detectors – just five very limited 3D senses (with a potential of a sixth sense – I will explain later) and these paltry senses have been further modified and restricted. No wonder we can hardly 'see' anything in the unfathomable vastness of Creation. The Earth and our existence is a single grain of sand out of the all deserts and beaches on a million, million Earth-like planets put together. So please do not think we are alone and our planet is special and unique, and our 3D 'scientific' and physics discoveries are of any significance anywhere except on lowly 3D Earth, because I assure you they are not!

Whatever your viewpoint is up to now, let's just suppose that you are with me so far, regardless if you simply cannot - or will not, believe any of this 'stuff' I am telling you, or you are still very sceptical. Let's also suppose you can accept (or pretend to for now) that there *must* be a multitude (inadequate word) of extra-terrestrial and inter dimensional life forms in the 'Omniverse' (the collective noun for all the universes and dimensions in existence) so is it not possible, probable, in fact out-and-out inevitable, that some of these Beings have visited the Earth over the eons? The chances of this *not* happening are so minuscule as to be totally negligent. So, if you can accept that Extra Terrestrials *must* have visited our Earth at some time (and many even taken up residence) I would suggest that it is also likely that not all the Extra Terrestrial visitors to our planet have been benevolent. Indeed, some have been downright malevolent and these visits are where things started to go seriously wrong for human life.

PERCEPTION IS REALITY.
SO IF WE WERE TO CHANGE OUR
PERCEPTION, THEN WE MUST
CHANGE OUR REALITY

13
The Annunaki

Going right back to the seeding of life on Earth our beautiful and bountiful planet has been regarded with envy among many Extra Terrestrial Entities, and for their own agenda, many of them have interacted with, and totally changed, the 'original' plan /design for life on Earth.

As we have agreed (if you can accept the *substantiated* assumptions, into your belief system, regarding the infinitesimal/none possibility that life in all the Universes is limited only to Human Beings on planet Earth) there are countless races and civilisations of Extra Terrestrial Beings in existence - and most of these are far more advanced than us Humans. Many of these Beings have visited Earth - and why wouldn't they want to visit such a wonderful planet once the 'seeds' of life were sown here and the atmosphere supported all kinds of wonderful plants and animals and an abundance of natural resources.

According to many legends and beliefs arising from knowledge passed down through generations, over the millenary and corroborated by artefacts, geological finds and people 'channelling' information from Higher Entities there was a race of super Extra Terrestrial Beings living on this world. Many people believe (myself included) that these Beings were similar to the Na'vi (as portrayed in the movie "Avatar" – ah, now there's a 'coincidence'?) they could telepathically communicate with the animals and plants and with the universal 'ocean' of consciousness and knowledge, they were a race of spiritual, high vibrational and loving people – who were what all we Humans should be like today. They cared about Earth and the wondrous gifts of nature, and life on Earth at that time was truly paradise. David Icke, in his phenomenal book '**The Perception Deception**' offers a detailed summary of this era in the history of Earth, if you are interested.

There were also many other advanced Extra Terrestrial visitors to Earth during that time and as highly sophisticated as they were, they never-the-less coveted many of the rare and precious resources bestowed to this planet. One of these visitors was a race of Extra Terrestrials called the Annunaki, who came for the huge deposits of gold found on Earth. After a long, catastrophic and debilitating inter-space war, the Annunaki needed vast amounts of gold to turn into powder (nano-gold) to plug the gaps in the partly destroyed atmosphere of their own planet and to help with the regeneration of their bodies (nano gold is an excellent nutritional supplement for Humans too). To mine and produce enough gold for their needs it would have taken a huge army of Annunaki, instead of the relatively small 'landing party; they had.

Of course they couldn't use the services of the advanced civilisations already living on Earth, who would have railed against an invading force coming to plunder their adopted planet. So instead they used various 'test-tube', cloning and genetic modification techniques - and physical interbreeding at times - to modify the existing indigenous humanoids to create a 'slave race' of 'Humans' to mine the gold for them. These humanoid creatures are known today as Yeti or Big Foot, and they still exist in many parts of the world (they have not evolved into man – or any other species, over all the hundreds of thousands of years – ah, another blow for Darwin). Humanoids – as well as all the different animals (including dinosaurs) and plants on Earth, were the result of seeding – different genetic codes introduced onto the planet, and not as 'evolution' (change) from a single genetic code.

Obviously the Annunaki required hard working and relatively intelligent, but docile beings, who could understand and obey orders and who could communicate and think for themselves (a little) to enable them to solve basic technical problems. However they did not want a being as sophisticated as themselves. Hence the fact that Humans have so much so-called 'Junk DNA', unused to this day, and are capable of using only 10% of brain capacity. This was the original design for Human slave labourers – ah, not much has changed since then and we are still (as yet) 'slave-labourers', but with a patently false perception that we are free, that we have free choice and freewill. Can anything be further from the truth? How can we have freewill and free choice if we don't even know what reality really is?

There is a vast amount of evidence to support this chronicle of the Annunaki– much of it can be interpreted from the Bible no less, the Annunaki are the misinterpretation of the 'God' who made man (in the image of himself) and Earth. And then there are the accounts of these Beings recorded on the ancient 'Sumerian Tablets'. There is also a huge, vast, humongous, magnitude of physical artefacts left behind on Earth by the Annunaki, not least the millions of 'stone walls' and 'pathways' found all over the Southern parts of the continent of Africa – where the gold was mined, and which were an energy generating complex, perhaps to, among other things, power mining tools and energy vortexes to 'export' the gold off the planet. The Pyramids and Stonehenge and many of the other, inadequately explained, monolithic structures scattered about Earth are also all likely to be courtesy of the Annunaki or other off world Entities. These structures were certainly *not* built by ancient Egyptian slaves or cavemen as the fairy stories in (mainstream) history books would try to have you believe.

Micheal Tellinger's book "**The Slave Species of god**" explains the history of the Annunaki and the formation of Human Beings in great detail, and with unalienable evidence. 'Unalienable', that is, if your imposed belief system will *allow* you to believe it. This gives rise again to the question – what is knowledge? Knowledge is simply your belief system, which has been shaped and programmed by dogma, religion, education, or god-forbid, the (highly controlled and suppressed) mainstream sciences and documentaries. When dealing with subjects which are beyond normal 3D, third dimensional (basic left brain) thinking you will never expand your knowledge (or alleviate your self-imposed ignorance) without an open, even if sceptical, mind. Don't roll your eyes and think, that this is all just unbelievable nonsense as a knee-jerk reaction (simply because it is more convenient and 'safe' for you to do so) without due consideration, some critical thinking... and some research of your own.

14
Things get Complicated

I have just covered in in a few paragraphs, what Micheal Tellinger and many others have taken huge books and publications to explain, but the point of this treatise is to communicate the *basic* circumstances of how mankind was developed and to go towards answering the questions who we are and what we are. Further information and convincing proof of my assertions can be found elsewhere, with a little research.

The Annunaki, like many races of Beings, had benevolent and malevolent factions among them. The story of the Annunaki on Earth is basically about two brothers who were responsible for the gold mining operations here. One brother developed an affinity with the new Human race that he had helped to create and develop, while the other brother, maintained a disdain and contempt for them. To cut a long (although interesting, but for now unnecessary) story short the rivalry between the brothers, and other issues, eventually ended in a cataclysmic event that is described in the Bible, and in many other religious and traditional scripts, as the 'Great Flood'. As a result of this disastrous phenomenon, which wiped out most of the life on Earth, including the advanced civilisations (including Atlantis) and most of the

Annunaki's fledgling Human race, there was virtually a clean slate for life to start again. The tsunamis' and floods also totally altered the Geo-structure of the planet, sank islands, created new mountains and canyons and buried vast areas of previous civilisations. According to the Bible (and many other ancient scripts) 'Noah' built an Ark to survive the flood and save as much life as he could. This symbolises the act of the Annunaki, warning their 'chosen' Humans about the coming flood and collecting and saving animal and plant DNA prior to the disaster.

With a clean slate the surviving Humans were reduced to cavemen and planet Earth became rife with Extra Terrestrial life of all kinds. Some only visiting, but quite regularly, others who became resident on the planet, and still are! Some of the different races of ETs and their interactions with Humans are responsible for the different races of Humans on Earth today. Asians did not develop from Asian apes, nor Europeans from Caucasian ones! Among the many ETs were the Nepholim (Giants) who had a big influence on the development of the Ancient Egyptian culture for example. *All* Human Beings are human/ET hybrids. It is widely agreed that humanity is the result of interactions with as many as twelve different ET races. However, by far, the biggest determinant on the further development of Humans (and on other ET races on Earth also) was a highly malevolent Universal inter-dimensional entity known by many different names by different cultures, but I''ll call them the Demons (as named and described in the Bible). These Demons or Archons, another well used name for them, could well have been an influential factor in the more evil factions of the Annunaki as well, and in the *'creation'* of the great floods, for their own future agenda.

The Demons/Archons were certainly the 'masters' of a race of inter dimensional Reptilian entities, who in turn became the masters of the Human race by interbreeding with Humans and creating a bloodline of 'Pharaohs, Kings, Queens' and rulers that have exerted dominant control over the Human race since then – and still do today. "Yes, Your Majesty"...come on, think about it – who gave the UK Queen, or any Queen, the right to be a 'majesty? I certainly didn't! They are not superior to me (or you) in any way. The Royal family of the UK – and the surviving monarchies of Europe and elsewhere, are all of 'Reptilian' decent and have hybrid DNA, as do most of the super-rich Jewish families, who are systematically collecting the all the World's wealth today. The existence of Reptilian entities is easy to establish. David Icke became famous (infamous) and universally derided and pilloried for his outspoken views on 'Reptilian' bloodlines, especially as related to the British Royal family. However time and again his perceptions, from his tireless research, have been vindicated. And one only has to look at the massive (inadequate word) amount of reptilian, snake and dragon symbolism used throughout history and throughout the world, in all cultures, and to learn about the functions of the 'Reptilian' (part of the) brain to see the connections – Ah, unless you think it's all just 'coincidence'. Yeah right!

I once had a student who wrote an extended essay titled "Is the Dragon the Most Depicted Icon in all History?" Her conclusion was - yes it is, but she didn't find out why. At the time I wondered about the reasons for this myself.

It was only later that I began to see all the connections. The Dragon and Reptilian symbolism all over the world has all come from somewhere, it did not just appear for nothing or by chance. It all refers in some way or other back to the Demon/Archon infested Reptilian entities who are influencing, through their hybrid/human 'puppets', virtually everything on Earth. As with most knowledge the *truth* of it is there to see, in plain view, if we really look and try to understand it. Simon Parkes, a political councilor from the UK, was in fact raised by Reptilian beings, he is a hybrid Reptilian/Human. He escaped being a part of the demonic influences normally prevalent in Reptilian races. His story is fascinating, and very credible due to his clearly down-to-earth and intelligent character.

So now we have on our hands, in our minds, a vicious and pestiferous inter-dimensional virus like entity, infecting the 'Elite' (who control us) and controlling them, and using them for their own hideous and malevolent agenda. The demonic Archons lead by their Demiurge, Satan, the Devil and their puppet Reptilians, are responsible for *all* the evil in the world today.

The Demon's influence is not just limited to the Reptilian races (of which most are not inherently evil and would not be, except for their Demonic infestation and control) and their hybrid 'puppet' Humans. But also each one of us individually can be effected by the Demons/ Archons to a lesser or greater degree. The Demonic influence manifests itself in many ways. At one extreme psychopaths and murderers, paedophiles, rapists and all manner of violent criminals are likely to be as much a victim (of uncontrollable Demonic urges) themselves as the people they perpetrate against. At the other level 'road rage', atypical outbursts, irrational feelings of fear and anxiety and unthinking (and instantly regrettable) violent reactions are all symptoms of Demonic induced behaviour. Knowing this, and accepting it, can create a degree of protection for oneself. In circumstances of deep stress, take a deep breath or two, count to ten and try to stop for an instant to think before reacting. Think of the Demons/Archons as the 'Devil' on your shoulder, whispering in your ear, because that is exactly what it is, and try to counter negative, dense and low vibrational responses. Impossible at times I appreciate, but realising what is happening will help towards mitigating the effects of your negative Demonic urges and feelings.

I'm only responsible for what I tell you – not for what you understand....

15

Things Went Wrong

As well as Earth the Demons/Archons have 'infected' many other planets and ET civilisations throughout the Universes. They are like an insidious virus 'feeding' off the base emotions (fear, anger, aggression) of physical beings and deliberately causing situations and circumstances to promote these emotional states in order for them to thrive and to bring about control and domination of whatever species they are infecting. The Demons have no natural 'Human' traits - empathy, love, compassion, imagination, creativity – however they have bestowed upon Humans many of their traits – cold-blooded behaviour, robotic and mechanical thought, anger, power - the need to dominate (over others) and, in many cases...just *pure* evil. Indeed at the very top of the Demon hierarchy is the 'Demiurge' – The Devil, Satan, if you like.

It is not an exaggeration to say that the Demon Demiurge - Satan (Satanic) worship is the real foundation of all Religions. Of course the millions upon millions of religious followers of all kinds have no idea about this, but never-the-less religion is simply a form of mass mind-control and the leaders of the religions *know this*. An interesting fact *ALL* Catholic Popes (in recorded history) have had to go through a satanic initiation ceremony/process before they can become Pope, which involves the sacrificial killing of a human baby and drinking his/her blood. *What*? I just don't believe that mate. I promise you I have not written that lightly or without conviction – there is enough evidence and corroborated testimony to justify my confidence in it being the truth. Also, after as much research as I have done, and connecting all the 'dots' (different pieces of the puzzle) it actually makes perfect sense that this should be so. Catholicism, as all religions, is based on the worship of a false God. "Amen" (said at the end of prayers) is, in fact another name for the Devil. The Pope leads the worship of the Devil and he is heavily Demon influenced. The 'energy' derived from the blood sacrifice of a baby, not only energizes a new Pope, but also confirms his allegiance to the Demons. However, believe that or not...not, if you need to hang on to the otiose comfort of your current belief system, it is painfully obvious to anyone with any intellect that 'Religion' has caused far more human suffering and destruction over the millennia than it has doing good for humanity. Which sounds a lot like Satanism to me – and whether you accept it or not, this is all due to the influence of the Demonic Archons and Reptilians over Human Beings.

Another thought to ponder – 'owning' over 1/6 of the land mass on the planet and being worth in excess of 50 Trillion £ the Queen of England could end all famine and poverty in the whole world tomorrow, if she so desired (as a true 'Christian' would – surely?) and still have a greater fortune left than any 'normal' Human could ever spend in many lifetimes. But, alas this thought has simply never entered her head. She would rather hoard her gold and jewels and land assets and live off the UK tax payer than contribute to the benefit of mankind. Hmm, sounds a bit Satanic to me. In fact it is actually much worse than that, she (the Queen) is head of the (Reptilian/Demon influenced) Global Cabal that is actually effectively contributing to *ensure* famine and poverty prevails in the world. (Poverty is control). The Queen, and other members of the Royal family, also take part in Satanic rituals involving the sacrificing of Human children and drinking their blood. The demon influenced Reptilian part of them thrive on the low dense energy given off by a child's fear, horror and pain as they are butchered. The Queen and her extended family, and other evil families, mentioned in a moment', are the non-human Humans I was referring to earlier. They are the direct bloodline descendants of the Demon controlled Reptilian race and they are hybrid Reptilian/Human creations. This is why it is so important to the Royal (why am I spelling it with a capital R?) families of the world to inbreed amongst themselves, arranged marriages between cousins, nephews and aunts etc. to maintain the Demon Reptilian/Human bloodlines. There are also a great many more of these hybrids, all around the world in all walks of life, usually in tight control of something or other.

Have you ever been tempted to give, or have given, money to charity, to help 'feed a hungry child'? Of course you have (you're human) I have. I have made lots of donations to various charities in the past mindlessly thinking I am doing my bit to end poverty. The regular adverts on TV, which cost thousands of dollars to make incidentally (good profits there for some one!) inducing us to give up some of our money to help the needy leave me totally cold nowadays.

These charities really are just another way of transferring wealth – not from the poor to the even poorer, but from the relatively poor to the already mega-rich. In hardly any case does any money get to where the adverts say it's going. All along the way, so many people are getting a 'cut' from it, the charity leaders/controllers, distribution organisations, local governments, red-tape and other unnecessary bureaucracy etc. that there is virtually nothing left for the 'poor' people at the end. The already mega-rich of the world could end *all* Human poverty with one stroke tomorrow, if they so desired, without any noticeable impact on their detestable wealth. Instead it is their avowed intention to create and maintain desperate poverty throughout the world, so I assure you any contribution you make (to most charities) is totally pointless and a complete waste of your money – and indeed often has the effect of actually helping to enable the mega-rich to create even more poverty (your own). Poverty is dependency and dependency is control. "Charity begins at home" is (unfortunately) an apt message in today's world and one you should heed.

Although the Queen of England is undeniably near the top of the control pyramid (just under the infected Reptilian Race and all influencing Demons/Archons – with the Demiurge – Satan, right at the top) she is, by a long way, not the richest of the World's ruling Cabal. That dubious honour goes to the senior members of the Rothschild family – estimated to own as much as 70% of the monetary wealth of the whole world. It is a long story how the Rothschild family became so rich and powerful and in control of the world (of course under the direct influence of the Reptilians/ Demons) in less than 200 years and I will not tell it here - but the information is all just a Youtube search away. Search in Youtube 'Richest family on Earth'. The Rockefeller family are not far behind – along with other Jewish moguls such as the JP Morgan dynasty the Schiff and the Harriman families and others. These are the 'people' who are in total control of the planet by proxy. How did they manage to get into this position of such power and control?...Of course, money!

Imagine that you own – that is you and your extended family, own, or have majority shares in, *all* the major banks in the world (the Rothschild's have). There are only three countries on the planet that do not have a Rothschild owned or controlled central bank. And imagine you can simply print (like a forger) as much 'money' as you want, without having any physical assets of value (Gold) to back it up. You can simply print pieces of paper, and put any denomination you want on them, at will. Then you 'lend' these pieces of paper to the governments of the world - with interest! Heck, nowadays you don't even have to print paper – just create numbers on a computer screen (bank accounts). And all these governments then 'waste' this 'money' on 'terrorist' security (there really are no bogey men Islam terrorists of course) or on wars, or on corruption to get into power, or on paying themselves and their cronies preposterous salaries, or on furthering the agenda of world control at the behest of the bankers, or whatever. Then they tax their populations to ensure that you get your money back with interest! How rich do you think that will make you? Virtually all the Income tax from most countries is used just to pay the interest accruing with the *privately* owned banks (not the capital as well, just the interest). So every country is always in your debt (power and control). Not only that, because you own so much of the 'money' in the world you can manipulate the Forex - Foreign Exchange markets, and the stock markets, and the 'futures' markets, heck, *all* the financial markets of the world, to make sure when you 'speculate' you never lose! How rich do you think that will make you? Not only that you own, or co-own, *all* the major corporations of the world and their (there isn't a suitable word in the dictionary to describe their obscenely astonishing amount of) profits. How rich do you think that will make you?

With the kind of money (power) that these families own it is not difficult (surely?) to see how they can own and control virtually everything on the planet. It is easy to confirm this is all true, *if* you want to? There is nothing that they cannot buy to further their agenda – which is total dominance of the whole planet and its entire population. The Queen and her family and other Royal families still clinging to 'power' around the globe and the Jewish/Zionist families already mentioned, between them own and control virtually the whole of the world's resources. The very free natural resources provided as a birth right to everyone born to this planet. They now *own* them...and we, in our ignorance, let that happen.

The world we live in *is* totally controlled by these people who have the most money (power and control) – this simply *cannot be* argued against with any *honest* intellectual integrity. These people who have more money (power and control) than anyone else can, and do, dictate what happens in life at every level. They control the main governments of the world, they control the main science and education systems of the world, they control the main financial corporations of the world, they control the main medical and pharmaceutical companies of the world, they control the main power (oil and nuclear) industries of the world, they control the main media (propaganda) outlets of the world, they control the main food production and farming of the world, they control the main entertainment (mind-control) businesses of the world and of course they control the main military industry of the world.

It is not a difficult task to find that this is all true – basic research on the Internet will reveal the names of the same few richest families in the world and their associates - virtually all of whom are Rothschild Zionists - turning up time and again linked at the very highest level with all of the above institutions - and is it just a coincidence that virtually all these people are Jewish? Let me say here I have nothing against Jewish people in general – I am sure that many of them are just like everyone else on the planet, hard-working, limited in perception, 'slaves'. However, since Biblical times the Jews have considered themselves as the 'chosen race' (yes, chosen by the Satanic Demons) and since then, whether by coincidence or not (there are no coincidences in life) Jewish people always seem to be the ones involved with the highest amounts of money and control at all levels in society...as we shall see...

Follow this link...to watch a highly informative documentary called "All Wars are Bankers Wars"...

https://www.youtube.com/watch?v=5hfEBupAeo4

Only fools call others crazy or stupid, due to their own lack of understanding...

16

The Protocols of the
Elders of Zion

*"The Protocols of the Elders of Zion" or
The Protocols of the Meetings of the Learned
Elders of Zion is an anti-Semitic hoax purporting to
describe a Jewish plan for global domination"...*

This is how that 'wonderful' (sarcasm) font of all (suppressed and controlled) knowledge 'Wikipedia' describes this heinous document...as an *anti-Semitic hoax...*? Oh, come on... Why would a *huge* document such as this - an outpouring of plans and ideas and strategies to take control of the world; "WORLD CONQUEST THROUGH WORLD JEWISH GOVERNMENT" (and ways to implement them) published in 1897, be written as a *hoax?* Search 'The Protocols of the Elders of Zion' on the internet and read these incredibly detailed writings – and then come back and tell me they were written as a *hoax!* (Oh, beam me up Scotty from this crazy mind-manipulated world) Pleaaase... even a modicum of critical thinking, would (surely?) suggest to you that *nobody* would go to that extent (particularly in 1897 when so few 'outside' people would actually see it) of writing such a tome, that would have taken an *immense* amount of time and imagination to even think about – let alone write out (painstakingly by hand) just for a 'hoax'...?

I realise that mankind has been (deliberately) dumbed-down over the years, but does Wikipedia, the (Jewish/Zionist) people who control it, really expect everyone to be obtuse enough to simply accept the explanation that it was just a hoax? Evidently they do. Go and read the (huge) Wikipedia explanation of this book, so that your belief system can be assuaged. You can agree and take comfort that Wikipedia's such detailed and convincing counter-account *must* be right – and I am wrong.....Ah! but, sorry to burst your bubble, there is one small thing – most of the 'protocols' detailed in the 'The Protocols of the Elders of Zion' have *already* taken place and have been implemented! So the book could hardly be a hoax, or do they want you to believe that *everything* that has happened (as described in the document) is just a coincidence, rather than the plan? Ah, we can tell the dumb public anything, most of them are just too anserine to give this - or anything, much thought. Just 'entertain' the masses and we can get away with whatever else we want...

Presumably they want you to believe that this book was perpetrated as a hoax to gain, what? Sympathy (?) for the poor down-trodden and victimised Jews – who just happened to own the most money (power and control) in the world at the time – and still do? Someone apparently had it in for the Jews pretty badly and wanted to malign them so much, and make out that they would even think of such a thing as trying to gain ever more money (power and control). Oh, surely not, not Jewish people. Well, if you believe all that, please contact me. I own a beautiful

Island in the South China Sea, my boy, and I will sell it to you, and then tell you where it is, after you have transferred $100.000 to my bank....honestly! Actually there is no way I would personally make such an outrageous claim just to fool you out of your money, money is not that important to me – but then again I'm not Jewish!...Oppps my bad, I just made another anti-Semitic comment. Ah, I know 'The Protocols of the Elders of Zion' was written as a Hoax so that Hitler, forty years in the future, could claim the 'hoax' publication was real and use it as an excuse to persecute the Jewish population of Europe...??? Hellooo....! (As suggested by Wikipedia - I kid you not).

I am very sorry to have used so much sarcasm in the last couple of paragraphs, but to me, the childish rubbish they can come up with makes me laugh. And the sheer contempt for your intellect (obviously they assume you have *none*) that the Zionist/Jewish controlled writers of Wikipeadia (and *all* other mainstream media) have for you is simply staggering. 'The Protocols of the Elders of Zion' *is* obviously a genuine and authentic document that *is the* basic blueprint that *has* been/*is* being followed, for (Jewish) domination of the world. You can read it (free) http://www.biblebelievers. org.au/przion1.htm (by using this url) After you have read it there is NO way that you will agree that this (very) long and brilliantly detailed writing explaining exactly the steps required to take control of the world, is anything except *genuine*. Or, of course, you can also totally ignore it and continue to believe (in your self-imposed ignorance) that there are no 'conspiracies' in the world. A bunch of Jews running the planet? What a laugh, what morons believe that? Only the stupid 'conspiracy theorists'. I have made no attempt to research for myself, other than in the highly (Zionist/Jewish) controlled mainstream, but I know the conspiracy theorists are all wrong and just stupid, because everyone else also thinks the same. (Ah, do some critical thinking here – *who* are the stupid ones?)

Of course not all Jewish people are collectively responsible for all the atrocities that the Zionist Jews have meted out on the world's population in their (on-going) quest for world domination. (A New World Order). Many Jews, as I have just suggested are just as hard working and limited in perception, 'slaves' as anyone else. And I am not anti-Semitic, I have no feelings one way or the other about this race of people, or is it a Religious group? The point I am making here is how easily duped most of the world's population can be (you?). The Holocaust, which plainly and clearly *IS* a hoax, is claimed by the Zionist Jews to be real. And 'The Protocols of the Elders of Zion' *ARE* obviously (to anyone with a 'free' mind) *genuine* and are claimed by the Zionist Jews to be a hoax...heck, they want it all ways! At the expense of your mental faculty (lack of). I understand you may not want to, or have the time to bother, but if you did and you started taking a little more notice of the world you are in, you would find out just how many Zionist Jews are in positions of power and influence (most behind the scenes) in the governments of the western world (and in fact most other parts of the world as well) and in control of all the major corporations and, of course, the mainstream media. If you do not research for yourself, then let me tell you – *a staggering* amount, and totally (and suspiciously) disproportionate to the general population. The amount of Jews in the world compared to all other races and creeds is obviously tiny – a few percent? But the Zionist Jews, an even smaller number, in positions of global power is probably close to ninety percent! Hmm, I wonder why? Luck, coincidence? Surely it can't be the result of a well thought out, devious, and impeccably implemented *plan* – such as that *exactly* described in 'The Protocols of the Elders of Zion'!

I go back here to the premise that these Zionist Jews, who clearly *are* in control of the world, are demoniacally influenced. They are hybrid Demon/Reptilian/Humans, they *are* the 'chosen' race. Chosen, not by any religious God, as they would like to have you believe, but 'chosen' - infected by Satan and the Archontic Demon Aliens. These Aliens' have had the agenda for a totally repressed and controlled world population from their very first infection of Human

Beings (and other Entities) on Earth. This has been described in the Bible no less, and in other traditional, religious and influential books. And since that time Mankind has always had to battle against their 'Demons'. Unfortunately, due to the lower and denser vibrations of Earth during these times, the Demons/Archons have been easily able to gain the upper-hand (they feed and thrive on low dense vibrational energy) and to manipulate and create events to shape the world into how they want it. The dear old 'Elders of Zion' are as much victims as the rest of us. They are the *chosen* 'puppets' and they have been deceived/infected into thinking they are the 'chosen ones' to lead humanity (down the toilet). The only difference is they have become super-rich doing it! A full, highly readable, explanation of the history of International Jewry and how they came to such power can be found in the very informative book by Belton Bradberry **"The Myth of German Villany"**

Unfortunately for the Archon/Demons and their puppet Zionist Jews and bloodline Royal families, the vibrations of Earth are getting increasingly higher and less dense and this is causing the 'enlightenment' of more and more people each day. The more people who are enlightened, 'waking up' to what is going on all around them, the less dense energy there will be for the Demons to feed on (leading to their demise) because the more enlightened a person is, the higher their vibrations (energy) become. Do you think it is just a coincidence that the word dense is often used referring to people who are 'thick', stupid...unenlightened?

It all starts making complete sense, if you tax your brain with some critical thinking. The Bible (and other religious books) tells the story of the 'Demons' (Fallen

Angels) obviously in a more emblematic and symbolic way than I do here, and the Jews are described as the 'chosen' ones to lead humanity (New World Order). 'God' (symbolic of the Annunaki) created man in his own image. Adam and Eve and the 'serpent' (Reptilian Being). Noah's Ark and the flood - the Demonic and intentional wiping out of advanced civilisations...and on it goes. There is so much of *true* reality told in religious texts, but these have, down the eons, been (purposely) misinterpreted into a 3D left-brained, religious, doctrine. Read it with a different view, an open-mind and interpretation, and the Bible can verify much of what I have postulated here in this book. Follow this link to hermeneutics expert Peter Kling if you are interested in finding out many more interpretations of the Bible and its prophecies. Totally fascinating. http://www.peterkling.com/

You'll never leave where you are – until you decide where you'd rather be.

17

All History is Wrong

It is said that the 'winners' write history, which really is another way of saying – the people who control the money are the ones who write the history, because they are *always* the 'winners' in any conflict or circumstance. It hardly matters what historical period you study, going right back to the beginning of chronicled events, virtually everything you have been taught is false. I could go through practically every major event and a great many not so major, that have shaped the history of the world throughout time, and factually contradict the accepted 'stories'. But, as with many subjects I am covering in this thesis, I would have to write a huge book to do so. And I have no need to do this because the book has already been written by the author and researcher John Hammer. "**The Falsification of History**" is a painstakingly investigated publication and every falsehood of reported history John Hammer has uncovered and rectified is substantiated with evidence and fact. I will however go through a few historical misconceptions here to highlight for you the claim that all history is wrong, and to explain some reasons why.

If you control the world you don't want people to know that you do – otherwise, of course you cannot have control over anything. So when the 'controllers' of the world cause and concoct events to change the geopolitical structure of the globe to their advantage, or manipulate a course of action to increase their wealth (power and control) they make sure, through propaganda and deceit and gullible, mind-controlled, or blackmailed, historians and reporters, that their own made-up version of events gets written and accepted.

Most of the monumental events of the past (and many others not so significant) have been deliberately engineered for a specific purpose. They have not been simply coincidental or circumstantial happenings that lead to a chain of other circumstantial events that then caused an impulsive reaction, or ill-considered course of action. This is what the 'controllers' of the world want you to think. Knowing what I do now (after extensive panoptic research) it makes me laugh when historians, and others, wring their hands and bemoan the failings and the betise of Human Beings in allowing these catastrophic events of the past to unfold. "The most important thing about knowing our history is so we do not make the same mistakes again!" is the customary claim of historians to valuate their subject. How often they simply blame the incompetence of leaders as explanations of why an event happened. Most of the time there were no 'mistakes' made at all, very rarely has there been a situation where 'man's folly' has caused anything significant. Both the World Wars, for example, were deliberately orchestrated for specific 'New World Order' (the dominance and control of the world) agendas. They did not come about because of a series of unfortunate and contemporaneous happenings, nor the ravings of psychopathic despots, as the history books want you to believe. Jealousies and rivalries between states and countries were deliberately inflamed, or even created, and false-flag events and despicable propaganda was copiously used by the world-controlling Jews (Elders of Zion). This is a very long story and not crucial to the thrust of my redaction, and the truth can be found and researched if you want it - "The Real Truth about WW2" is a good place to start on Youtube.

Basically both World Wars, and for that matter virtually every other war in modern history, were financed and fuelled by the parts of the Zionist Jewish Bank Cabal that controls the world. Hitler far from being the demonised figure of popular fiction (history and text books) was, in fact, a man of peace and no one tried harder to avoid war than him. Come off it – he was the biggest psychopath in history! How very convenient that assumption is for the *real* sociopaths who started the war. Hmm...an excellent cover story to deflect the truth. Hitler wanted only to secure the sovereignty and the prosperity of Germany that he, thanks to his brilliant statesmanship, had brought about after the diabolical and devious (but quite intentional) calamity which was the Versailles Treaty after the First World War. Mike King's excellent book "**The Bad War**" - the Truth about World War 2, details the *real* culprits who caused this world altering conflict...International Jewry.

Contentious or not, it is worth pointing out here, and highly relevant to this essay, that paradoxically it was actually Zionist/Communist Jews who brought about the ill-treatment and murder of the Jews during the 2nd World War. Hitler was actually very tolerant of the 'troublesome'

Jews in Germany at the time. The 'Holocaust' as popular 'fiction' (mainstream History and text books) would have it certainly did not happen. Granted there were a great many deaths in German detention camps of Jewish people and other enemies of Germany through disease, malnutrition and physical abuse, indeed perhaps even sick eugenics experiments, but NO Jews were gassed at Auschwitz. Certainly nothing like six million Jews were killed – or is it three million or two million, or one million? The authorities cannot make up their minds about how many Jewish deaths they can claim without more people becoming suspicious of the 'fairy story'. Today, and ever since the end of the War, Germany and America pay millions of dollars every year to the Zionist Jews of Israel in supposed reparations for the Holocaust...how expedient for them. Also, how convenient is it for the Zionist Jews to trot out the old "Holocaust" line every time they themselves commit atrocities, against Palestine for example, ah, after what happened to our people we have the right to 'defend' ourselves. Yeah, right! Of course I can now be called a Jew hating anti-Semitic but, there is enough evidence and *proof* (obviously suppressed and opposed in the mainstream) that the 'Holocaust' in simple practical terms, if nothing else, could *not* have happened. So me being called anti-Semitic, by anyone, is puerile to say the least. A simple search on Youtube – 'The Holocaust Hoax', will reveal enough evidence to sway any open-minded person towards the view that gassing that many people in the circumstances described and accepted, simply was not physically possible. The great book "**The Holocaust Hoax Exposed: Debunking the 20th Century's Biggest Lie.**" by Victor Thorn will also furnish you with (undeniable) proof of this monstrous fraudulence and an explanation as to how and why it came about.

> The alleged "Holocaust" of 6 million Jews at the hands of Adolf Hitler and National Socialist Germany during WWII is one of the most egregious and outrageous falsehoods ever perpetrated against mankind. Deceitful Jewish propagandists and their lackeys in the educational establishment, media, and Hollywood have foisted upon the world a completely baseless, manufactured narrative, chock full of a wide variety of ridiculous claims and impossible events, all to advance the Jewish agenda of world domination and subjugation. The official "Holocaust" story has been used to justify the very existence of the criminal, terrorist Jewish state occupying Palestine, garner public sympathy for Jews and elevate "Jewish suffering" above all others, and to reinforce the false narrative of historical Jewish persecution at the hands of "evil, irrational anti-Semites" who hate Jews. Organized Jewry has used the false "Holocaust" story to seize and distort our collective history for their corrupt ends, to demonise Adolf Hitler and National Socialist Germany specifically, and nationalism and European civilization generally. It is, without a doubt, the Big Lie of the 20th century.

British (independent) historian David Irving is actually offering – and has been for many years, $1,500.00 to anyone who can provide any documented proof that Hilter ordered (or even wanted) the gassing of any Jews. This reward still remains unclaimed!

There really can be no denying that the world and mankind *is* controlled and ruled over, by an 'Elite' of

Archon/Demonic/Reptilian bloodline families and Zionist Jews. Even if you cannot, or do not want to, believe in Extra Terrestrials or Alien entities being involved (due to your 'programmed' belief system) it is painfully obvious to anyone who looks up from 'American Idol' or their celebrity, or sports-star worship for even just a few minutes, that governments around the world are not working for the best interests of humanity, or for the interests of the people who supposedly elected them. Otherwise why is the world in such a mess...crashed economies, austerity measures, unemployment, poverty, homelessness, famine, disease, pollution, endless bloody wars and, of course, *uncontrollable* (?) 'Terrorism' (the catch-all convenient excuse for the ever increasing loss of civil liberties) etc. Come on, it is not merely man's folly or imbecility causing these things - it is the 'people' in charge pulling-the-strings of government 'leaders' who are *creating* them. And don't tell me that it's just the incompetence of certain unfortunate politicians, because after 'electing' new ones nothing ever gets better (usually gets even worse). *All* government leaders are controlled and told what to do by the people with the most money (power) and these people have an agenda to ensure that mankind's plight remains a struggle and a distraction to hide the real truth about what is really going on. At least 95% of all acts of 'terrorism' are induced by agents of governments (CIA, MI5, Mossad etc.) to cause conditions (false-flag) for the furtherance of the Demon agenda (the control of the population of Earth). *EVERY* time you see or hear of a 'terrorist' attack (anywhere in the world) be-headings etc. be sceptical....*very* sceptical! All is not what it may seem.

So, with that said, it is not so much of a stretch for one's mental faculty to comprehend historical events having been deliberately manipulated for various self-serving reasons. David Icke calls it 'problem-reaction-solution'. Cause a problem so that the population reacts in horror, or outrage, or fear, and then provide the 'solution' – which just happens to be the very outcome that was planned and desired in the first place. The classic illustration of this in action is the 'false-flag' event, aided and abetted by voluminous propaganda. There have been thousands of these throughout history.

A prime example of a false-flag event leading to problem-reaction-solution, is the attack on the Twin Towers of the World Trade Centre in New York on 9/11 2001 supposedly by Muslim 'Terrorists' (haha). The 'problem' was – the ruling Cabal, to further their powers of control, wanted the population (of most of the world) to get ever more accustomed to losing privacy and freedoms and get used to insidiously increasing measures of surveillance and dominance and to accept these as a part of their daily lives (easier to control). The 'reaction' (by the public) was shock, horror and fear and people demanded that governments, and other agencies should protect them from 'Terrorists'. The 'solution' of course, was the desired course of events that was planned for in the first place. More surveillance cameras *everywhere,* all sorts of new powers being introduced for harassing and arresting people on specious charges (people who do not toe the government's line), the (ridiculous and laughable) ever accelerative and invasive airport security checks and of course the never-ending 'war on terror' - which gives a convenient excuse for implementing absolutely any desired restrictions on freedoms and human rights. And, of course, the excuse to bomb, raid and invade other countries for Geopolitical reasons in the name of fighting 'terrorism' - oh, and steal their resources and oil while they're at it.

I am not going to go into all the ins and outs of the 9/11 attacks – as much information as you want (or want to avoid) about the real perpetrators of the attacks and the specific reasons for them, and how they were carried out, is *everywhere* on the Internet. I will say here though the 'official' story (fairy tale) of commercial planes hi-jacked by amateur 'Muslim Terrorists' being flown into the towers and the resulting explosions and burning fuel causing the catastrophic collapse, that we all witnessed on TV, is just totally absurd and ludicrous. I am sorry, but seriously, if you still need to (desperately) cling on to a belief system that has you going along with the mainstream reporting of this event, then I would suggest you are either just totally apathetic, or so completely 'programmed' or 'dumbed' down by group-think and TV that another episode of 'The X Factor' or 'The Next Supermodel' or whatever, is your only recourse. The collapse of the Twin Towers (two of the strongest buildings in the world) *and* nearby buildings, simply could not have been caused by a fire, however fierce, at the top of these super-strong structures, regardless of what you have been lead to believe.

In her book "**Where did The Towers Go**" Doctor Judy Woods (a former Professor at Clemson University, USA, with degrees in Civil Engineering, Mechanical Engineering and Materials Engineering Science) explains in great detail what really happened on 9/11 and how it happened. With so many *proven* facts and observations, photographs, compelling evidence and '*genuine*' eyewitnesses, it is simply not possible to argue against her findings with any degree of intelligent integrity. You can also see several presentations by Dr Judy Woods on Youtube – just search 'Where did the Towers go?' The Twin Towers of the World Trade Centre were turned to dust by a direct energy weapon and the 'collapse' had nothing to do with airplanes or controlled explosions. Remember, everything, *everything* in creation is just a form of energy, so change the energy (vibrational frequency) and the apparently solid will change appearance and state – concrete and metal to dust. Not really too difficult to understand or believe. To go even further also lookup 'Richard D Hall' on Youtube, the brilliant and pertinacious researcher and presenter, who has all but proven that the airplanes did not even exist – they were simply holographic projections – as they say, the plot thickens...

FREETHINKERS

are those who are willing to use their minds without prejudice and without fearing to understand things that clash with their own customs, privileges or beliefs. This state of mind is not common, but it is essential for right thinking; where it is absent, discussion is apt to become worse than useless.

18
Agenda 21

If you think I have given you 'food-for-thought' and seriously challenged your belief system, so far, this next section comes with an admonition – Do not read this chapter if you are of a sensitive disposition, or you have no desire to face a harsh *reality*.

'Agenda 21' is the name given to the United Nations Conference on Environment & Development held in Rio de Janeiro, Brazil, 3 to 14 June 1992. You can read this official document Online - a simple Google search - "Agenda 21" - will reveal a great many websites appertaining to this monstrous and flagitious document. I have included here the list of the virtuous sounding chapters contained therein, but which each reveals, anything but beneficent plans for the development of mankind. This is a document, pure and simple, for the total domination of mankind.

Chapter 1 Preamble
Section I. Social and Economic Dimensions
Chapter 2 International Cooperation for Sustainable Development
Chapter 3 Combating Poverty
Chapter 4 Changing Consumption Patterns

All but three countries in the world have been 'tricked' or coerced into ratifying this Agenda which describes, in deceptive language, the nightmarish (inadequate word) plan of the 'New World Order'. A 'New World Order' being the epithet and goal of the ruling Elite cabal, who want a *new* 'World Order' in which they control and dominate every aspect of mankind's existence on Earth. Why, if as you say, these people already have such wealth and power do they want, or need, to go so far as to *totally* subjugate humanity to their will? Power to them is not complete until it is absolute. Remember these people are controlled and dominated by an evil race of inter-dimensional satanic Beings who want the Earth as their own in the condition that best suits them - total ruination and desolation. Remember their 'food' (sustenance) is the low vibrational energy created by Humans living in fear, desperation and abject despair.

Couched in Copernican and innocuous sounding, albeit unnecessarily wordy, prose this 'Agenda' basically apportions the blame of Global pollution and devastation of the planet to the general population (when, in fact it is the Cabal's doing entirely) and plans ways of combating this state of affairs, that they have deliberately caused themselves. Problem/reaction/solution. The main substance of their justification for enforcing world-wide draconian 'sustainability' measures is their fairy story about 'Global Warming'...oops change that (there is NO Global warming - proven) to 'Climate Change', caused by man-made pollution. Again, not being the main subject of my treatise here I will not go on and on about my total derision about man-made 'Climate Change' - just suggest you do your own, beyond the mainstream, research. A Youtube search <u>"The truth about Climate Change"</u> by Lord Munkton will render all the facts and information that you will need to be convinced that 'Climate Change' is an absolute, and devilishly contemptible, hoax, perpetrated with the sole intention of giving ever more control to the criminal ruling Cabal. Oh, and make them even richer through the ridiculous (ludicrous and funny - if it wasn't so serious) 'Carbon Tax'.

A tiny bit, so as to not tax your belief system too much, of critical thinking here will, surely (?) give you pause for thought about this. Co2 the purportedly main 'pollutant' contributing to "Climate Change" is vital to all plant life on the planet – there cannot really be too much of it...the more of it there is the more trees and plants will grow (if they were allowed to) and the greener Earth will become. And the quality of the air we breathe would get better (plants produce oxygen remember...?) The incessant, and planned *deliberate,* deforestation of the rain forests and the destruction of the fertility of the soil (GMO and pesticides and over intensive single crop commercial farming) are greater causes of the increasing Co2 on the planet than a few Chinese smoking factories, or you using too much oil-created energy ("carbon footprint" haha). If they were talking about any other man-made pollutants (and they're not) who is actually producing the waste-matter that is polluting Earth's atmosphere? Duh, the industrial corporations, who are all owned by the very same people who are responsible for writing Agenda 21! This has *nothing* to do with 'us', mankind/general population, polluting anything. Really 'Global Warming' is *absolutely totally fake* – it really is a joke and you should treat it as such. *Please*, for everyone's sake, do not be dumb and nescient enough take *any* part of the (comical – it really is) 'Climate Change' story seriously. There really is enough proof and *real* evidence available (as opposed to the faked and manipulated evidence of mainstream Zionist/Jewish-owned science) if you seriously look for it. And open your mind to the possibility that your belief system is being systematically programmed to believe that we (Humans) must give up all our individual rights to 'protect' our own planet from ourselves.

Our planet Earth is quite capable of looking after itself. It is a living, ever-regenerating, energetic entity that certainly does not require any 'sustainability' measures introduced by the criminal Demonic influenced ruling cabal, which will ultimately benefit them rather than mankind – or the planet. Again try a little critical thinking here...if *everyone* on the planet did something...I don't know what....stop breathing out Co2 for a few seconds? Switch off their electricity for a while, bought and used less petrol than normal? Bought a bike...whatever? Do you think it would really make any difference to the climate? Of course it wouldn't. Earth can cope with our 'pollution' easily. Now, if the Global Corporations (owned by the same people bemoaning and promoting the scourge of man-made 'Climate Change') stopped burning fossil fuels to create electricity, and 'found' alternates to petrol and gas (they exist already) and stopped incessant deforestation, and stopped their factories spewing out all sorts of toxic wastes everywhere, and stopped experimenting with ozone-damaging weather manipulation, that *might* make a difference. But of course they won't - too much profit to lose. They want *you* to give up *your* rights – to 'help' the planet, but they won't give up *anything*. So how does that help the climate? It helps nothing - except the controllers of the world to increase their control over you.

'Sustainability' is the key word in this grotesque deception of the population. Everything, all the atrocious plans, for the total mastery of the world's population in Agenda 21 relates to making everything more *'sustainable'* If you see this word in any document, or leaflet, or child's book, or classroom, or hear it on TV, in any program relating to geography or climate, simply roll your eyes, palm your face and sigh at the ridiculous and infantile attempt to fool you. Although it is like trying to push water uphill with some (mind-controlled, group-think) people, trying to inform others about this *seriously* fiendish plot is also a good idea. Humankind deserves better than to be treated with such utter disdain and contempt, by the proponents of 'Climate Change'. Of course some people in positions of responsibility (not *real* scientists who have done *genuine* research themselves though) fervently believe in the Climate Change myth, as earnestly reported to them, but most are paid or black-mailed to support this dupery - which, of course will backfire on them eventually as they too will be subjected to all the increased evil control methods supposedly justified by this fraud. We are back to money again and all the evil it causes. Scientists and reporters and 'government officials' all lying (maybe a *few* unknowingly?) about something as serious as this just to keep their jobs – and salaries!

Is there not *any* justification in trying to be responsible in our approach to making the planet more 'sustainable'? Surely without something being done our world will eventually be choked by man's thoughtless and needless pollution. You can argue that making something 'environmentally sustainable' must be a positive thing, but you have to look no further than at the people who are actually responsible for 'inventing' and introducing 'environmental sustainability' (Agenda 21) to realise the motivation behind this agenda is in no way benevolent. After some research you will find that it is the same Zionist Jewish 'puppets' (who are controlled by the Archons) who are also responsible for all the devastation caused by the monetary debt system, and the warmongering genocide (blamed on mythical terrorists) and all the other false-flag events that are necessary to create the conditions in the world for the introduction of a 'New World Order'.

Man's rubbish dumped in the ground and at sea and the careless and unnecessary use of plastic (for profit - and to taint food) is obviously a problem but is one that Mother Earth can cope with. Please think about the (deliberate) deadly radiation leaks and the chemtrails and deliberate heavy industrial pollution, and the deliberate deforestation of the Amazon jungle, before concerning yourself unnecessarily about all the (for sure untidy and hazardous, but not life-threatening) non-biodegradable litter around. I would rather live on a rubbish dump with clear skies above, than in a beautiful house and garden being constantly bombarded with highly toxic Chemtrails.

Regardless of the Agenda's pernicious plans to outlaw all private home and land ownership - *all* land on Earth will be 'owned' and controlled by the 'state' (the mega-rich Jews and bloodline Royal families) and introduce 'No-Go' areas for human inhabitation and activity, which will amount to 90% of the planet, and concentrate all housing into 'sustainable' (ha-ha that word again) hi-rise and high density 'cities', And the transfer of child-rearing to the 'state' (for mind manipulation) and the 'trans-human' mind control by micro-chip, and the 100% surveillance of *everyone* (these are all part of this documented Agenda! - read it!) By far the most scandalous and heinous part of the program is to cull the world population from seven billion people to a more *'sustainable'* (roll eyes again) 500 million people. Go away, that's simply not possible. Oh yeah? it certainly is, and it's going on right now! Google "The Georgia Guide-stones" and you will see that 'someone' has erected a modern stone monolith with the ten 'commandments' for a 'New World Order' written in ten different languages carved into it. And one of these 'commandments' is...'to maintain a *'sustainable'* population of around 500 million people', or words to that effect – see for yourself. No fiction writer, or movie producer, could ever make this up it would just be seen as too ludicrous – and this is exactly the idea, it is all so preposterous that no one will believe it or take notice of it. But this *is* our reality as we see and experience it now. And, just in case you are pondering a viewpoint that has any degree of sympathy to the idea that the world *is* becoming overcrowded...this is simply not true. The ever regenerating Earth can sustain a virtually unlimited amount of people who are living in peace and harmony and with love and respect for the planet. Nature, the perfect design of the Creator, would not allow overcrowding to occur anyway. The more enlightened a Being is, the more consideration to sensible birth control is given. Earth could be, and should be, a paradise – but there are also many other planets in the Universes that *are* paradise that the Souls of (former) Human Beings could also inhabit.

In September 2015 the 'Agenda 21' was revised and renamed 'The Agenda for 2030'

No longer is it an Agenda to be achieved by the 21st century – the Agenda now has been speeded up to be completed by 2030 - as the Archon influenced hybrid puppets desparately try to fight against the awaking higher vibrations of the planet. All the hienous control aims of Agenda 21 are still the ultimate accomplishment but now these aims have been disguised as '17 Goals' for *'sustainable development'*. These 'Goals' for the future 'sustainabilty' of mankind all sound wondrous and no one in their right mind could possibly object to them. Add to that a sustained propaganda campaign featuring celebrity 'dupes' (or are they paid-for, or black-mailed, puppets of the Cabal?) - and innocent children, all extolling the virtues of these 'essential' sounding, life-improving 'Goals', and the *wonderful and salutary* UN (United Nations) have a recipe for fooling and deceiving yet more 'sheeple' into going along with, and even supporting, this agenda for the furtherance of the domination they have over them!

Here are these Goals;

Goal 1) End poverty in all its forms everywhere
Goal 2) End hunger, achieve food security and improved nutrition and promote sustainable agriculture
Goal 3) Ensure healthy lives and promote well-being for all at all ages
Goal 4) Ensure inclusive and equitable quality education and promote lifelong learning opportunities for all
Goal 5) Achieve gender equality and empower all women and girls
Goal 6) Ensure availability and sustainable management of water and sanitation for all
Goal 7) Ensure access to affordable, reliable, sustainable and modern energy for all
Goal 8) Promote sustained, inclusive and sustainable economic growth, full and productive employment and decent work for all
Goal 9) Build resilient infrastructure, promote inclusive and sustainable industrialization and foster innovation
Goal 10) Reduce inequality within and among countries
Goal 11) Make cities and human settlements inclusive, safe, resilient and sustainable
Goal 12) Ensure sustainable consumption and production patterns
Goal 13) Take urgent action to combat climate change and its impacts
Goal 14) Conserve and sustainably use the oceans, seas and marine resources for sustainable developmen
Goal 15) Protect, restore and promote sustainable use of terrestrial ecosystems, sustainably manage forests, combat desertification, and halt and reverse land degradation and halt biodiversity loss
Goal 16) Promote peaceful and inclusive societies for sustainable development, provide access to justice for all and build

effective, accountable and inclusive institutions at all
levels

Goal 17) Strengthen the means of implementation and revitalize
the global partnership for sustainable development

How can anyone disagree with these? And that is the very idea behind them. What the Agenda 2030 document does *not* state however is how these 'Goals' will be achieved? Some more critical thinking here...take Goal number one, for example; if everyone is poor (apart from the ruling Elite) then reletive poverty has been irradicated. I know that sounds a bit simple and glib – but look at the way things are already going. Austerity measures, more and more taxes, more and more debt, more and more displacement of people (by manufactured wars and 'terrorist' attacks) more and more job losses and ever less money for social security services. The rape and control of all Earth's natural resources by the very same people responsible for the 'Agenda 2030' fraudulence.

What about 'Goal 2'; end hunger - by asserting control over all food production, which is what (one of the biggest – and nastiest, corporations in the world) Monsanto are already trying to achieve, with their GMO crops and *'patented'* (for goodness sake) seeds! No more natural seeds – just *manufactered* ones!? Are you kidding me!?

'Goal 3'; this one involves 'vaccines for health'. Making *ALL* vaccines mandatory for *EVERYONE*. Only *very* basic research will show, anyone who looks, that vaccines are far from being beneficial to health, except in the 'Alice in Wonderland' world of 3D 'reality', and of the UN controllers. Now, come on 'Goal 4' to anyone with a free mind, is a totally transparent control measure – inclusive and equitable '*education*' for all. Provided by who? Obviously by the 'government' – who are controlled by the Banking and Royal Boodline Cartel (who also happen to control the UN). In this situation 'education' will be little more than indoctrination.

I am sorry but *everyone* of the 'Agenda 2030' laughable *Sustainable Development Goals* are each simply a very thinly cloaked increased control measure, which all but the very dumb, single-minded and naive deniers will finally recognise.

For more information on this visit this URL...

http://www.naturalnews.com/051058_2030_Agenda_United_Nations_global_enslavement.html#ixzz3ozXnwCqg

19

Culling the Human Race

You mentioned the culling of the human race is already ongoing...Indeed it is and has been for a great many years. Of course all the 'manufactured' wars of the past few decades, for Geopolitical reasons – and for *profit*, have had the additional 'benefit' of reducing the population, as have all the 'manufactured' chemical diseases, such as Aids, Ebola and the plethora of introduced 'flu' viruses etc. Another big contribution to the 'culling' is vaccines. There is absolutely NO, ZERO *benefit to* having a vaccination. The science behind the idea of introducing a virus or disease, in small quantities, into a Human Being, to promote the production of 'antibodies' which may, in future, be able to stop or fight the disease, is totally and criminally (deliberately) flawed. Many private (not bought and paid-for mainstream) scientific studies have shown time and again that people who have been vaccinated against a disease are actually *more* likely to get it than others who have not been vaccinated. Because the so-called vaccine has done *nothing* except damage the body's natural immune system, and has compromised it's God-given ability to protect the human body, so that it cannot fight the very diseases the vaccines were supposed to protect against.

Please, even if you do not (cannot) believe a single word I have written so far, for the sake of your children's health, if not for your own, do some *serious* research about vaccines. Youtube is a good place to start – search "The truth about vaccines". Babies are given a great many, vaccines in the first few months of their life and the *ONLY* reason for this is to introduce natural immune system destroying chemicals and toxic metals into their bodies. These vaccines *will* cause illnesses and diseases in later life - be in no doubt about this - to the future profit of the medical and pharmaceutical industries, all owned by the same mega-rich Elite who design and promote the vaccines, and of course they will lead to an earlier than natural death (cull). Vaccines for children can also cause sterility in later life (a great way of 'sustaining' a reduced population) and they are absolutely known to be the cause of Autism and other mental anomalies. Do not ignore this information with a knee-jerk denial response, I simply would not make this up, nor would others. If you are a parent, or plan to be a one, you *owe* it to your child (future children) to take this paragraph *very* seriously. Find out about the highly poisonous brews that go into every vaccine.

Yes, I know you can cite that you have had vaccines in the past and you are OK. And I would answer, that when you had vaccines, as I did (not so many of them though in those days) the conditions on the planet were nowhere near as bad to health as they are now. Also I would question are you *sure* you are OK? High blood pressure? Forgetfulness? Easily susceptible to colds and flu? Coughs? Had any serious illnesses? A little asthma? Feeling older than you should? Stiff joints? Muscle aches and pains? All these symptoms, and many others, stem from a reduced immune system, damaged over the years by many things, but initially the rot was started with your vaccinations. I know many people will not want to even think about this, let alone do any research, ignore it and it will go away (how very ostrich). About now they are probably ruing not heeding my warning at the beginning about reading this book. However it is too late now to un-know this knowledge. On the other hand, although it might be a bit late-in-the-day, at least you can now ensure that no other vaccines are added to the toxic mess that our immune systems are being turned into. I can do nothing more than provide this *truthful* knowledge, what you do with it is your choice and freewill. Will you 'wake up', for the sake of your family, or not?

The totally Demonic influenced Bill Gates and his equally sinister wife of the Bill and Miranda Gates Foundation have already caused the suffering and deaths of countless thousands, perhaps millions, of children in Africa with his (*self-admitted* – I kid you not!) death-causing vaccines. Before you even think about shaking your head in disbelief put in the search box at Youtube "Bill Gates admits vaccines are used for Human depopulation". Ah, it is also interesting to note that he is one of the main champions of the Climate Change fallacy – he knows full-well that it is total BS but he probably thinks of himself as part of the Elite ruling Cabal and that he will benefit from 'doing his bit' for the 'New World Order'....ah sorry Mr. Gates, but in the end you are just as expendable as the rest of us to the Demonic Archons.

Working in concert with vaccines to destroy human health and create more future profit for the medical and pharmaceutical corporations, and to aid the 'culling', is the food industry. Virtually all food on the planet is being systematically poisoned. From the 'Frankenstein' toxic nightmare of GMO (Genetically Modified Organisms) food, to the deadly hormone drugged up livestock. *All* 'food' animals around the world *have* to be treated with hormones and other chemicals – ostensibly to improve the health of the animal, increase milk production, increase lean meat, make animals mature quicker, make animals more profitable etc. but bottom line, it is to make animals more noxious to Humans. From unnecessary, unnecessary that is unless you *want* to destroy health, poisonous food additives in virtually everything, to highly toxicant pesticides sprayed copiously (and unnecessarily) all over vegetable and fruit crops, to the over-use of highly poisonous refined sugar in modern manufactured food, virtually everything you eat is tainted in favour of an early death, or, at least, some nice profits from your inevitable ill health. Please do not waste your effort arguing with me here that your health is OK. A 'little' overweight are we? Playing tennis or squash two or three times a week, with no after effects? Prone to coughs, nasal congestion and flu and aches and pains? Perfect memory? The problem is you have no idea what perfect health really is, because you have never had it. But nature was designed with every conceivable *natural* nutriment a human body would ever need to ensure *perfect* health for a long (100 years plus) life and we have been deliberately robbed of the knowledge of most of them.

Another industry hell-bent on undermining human health is the water industry. In the 1950s Fluoride was added to the water supply of many countries around the globe, as a supposedly beneficial additive to improve the dental health of the population In reality Fluoride is an extremely toxic and hazardous substance – it is an industrial waste product from the aluminum and pesticide industries and would cost a fortune to dispose of safely and ethically. So let's get rid of it by simply dumping it in the water supply and telling people it is good from them. Ha, two birds with one stone – dispose of a highly dangerous waste product easily and without cost (in fact some water companies even pay for this hideous stuff to add to the water!) and also damage people's health towards the culling and for more future pharmaceutical profits. This is not made up! Research (Youtube) – 'The truth about Fluoride'...and make up your *own* mind - if your mind is free?

Another way the Demon influenced hybrid reptilian/ humans - the Royal families of Europe, particularly of Britain, the Rothschild's and Rockefeller's and their Zionist presidents and politicians and other associates and puppets, are going about their dastardly deeds to ensure a reduction (after a *profitable* bout of ill-health of course) in the population of the planet, is by systematically poisoning the atmosphere. If I mention 'Chem-trials' and evoke a blank look on your face, I can only say "Look up at the sky occasionally".

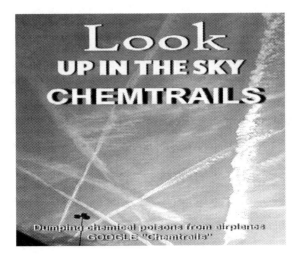

For the past ten years jets flying above normal airliner altitudes, have been spewing a noxious chemical brew of deadly (to life) heavy metals, chemicals and micro-organisms all over the skies of virtually every country on the planet. Ostensibly the trails of (can't think of a more suitable word) 'crap' that are being consistently sprayed all over the skies is to aid (here we go again) in controlling "Climate Change". Of course gravity – or more likely electro-magnetism (but that's another story) ensures that this heinous mixture falls to earth all over everyone.

Many people actually do notice these white trails emanating from high flying jets but just dismiss them as natural jet exhaust evaporation - con-trails. If more attention is paid to these trails though one will clearly see that Chemtrails take hours to disperse and then turn into hazy dirty looking whispy clouds, while con-trails disappear totally within minutes.

Wait, wait – if these Chemtrails have been sprayed on us for 10 years or so and they are as bad as you describe, why isn't most of the population already dead by now? Of course deaths of the old and frail caused by Chemtrails are not going to be publicised, but they are already happening in vast numbers. Also, as all the other methods of curtailing life early being used, Chemtrails have an accumulative effect, known as 'soft kill' (shortening of life over a prolonged period of time). People would, of course, smell a rat, if Chemtrails killed too quickly.

These Chemtrails also have other wonderful (if you are a Demon) benefits. Many Chemtrails contain nano technology particles that, when absorbed into the body and then into the brain can have an effect on mood and thought. They subdue and lower the natural energetic vibrations of the mind and can cause docility and suppress critical thinking. A mind-control technique to make people more easy to control, to get them to simply accept what is being forced upon them without rancor or even care. This would explain the distinct lack of questioning of this patent and monstrous daily phenomenon, or why so many people insist, against all awareness and obvious physical evidence, that Chemtrails are simply benign jet exhaust streams. To most people this is a safe and reassuring, although unmistakably false and uninformed, explanation. A quick note here; for most people who are 'awakened' (have a knowledge and understanding of what is *really* happening in this reality) Chemtrails have little, or no effect on them. Their higher natural energetic vibrations and surrounding aura, limit their intake of the Chemtrail particles.

Chemtrails can also be – and are (regularly) used in conjunction with the many HAARP systems around the world, not to change the climate, but to manipulate it! Oh, man is there no end to this tripe you are assailing me with? Controlling the weather now, oh, come on this is just getting crazy. Don't worry this is nothing, wait until I tell you that the Tsunami/earthquake that devastated Japan in 2011 and caused the nuclear power plant at Fukishima to fail, was caused *deliberately* – it was not a naturally occurring event. Ah, I am not reading any more of this you *are* crazy, or totally delusional! Who would ever do that, and why? Of course you are entitled to your opinion – and perhaps, if that is it, you ought to go now and see what's on TV, Go and get a good dose of *fictional* news from the - bought and paid for - BBC or CNN or Fox News, or whatever network you watch. Meanwhile for those people still here and want a *provable* explanation, it is in the next section...

It is one of the commonest of mistakes to consider that the limit of our power of perception is also the limit of all there is to perceive.

20

HAARP

"HAARP or High Frequency Active Auroral Research Program is an ionospheric research program jointly funded by the US Air Force and the US Navy. Designed and built by BAEAT (BAE Advanced Technologies) its purpose is to analyse the ionosphere and investigate the potential for developing ionospheric enhancement technology for radio communications and surveillance. The HAARP program operates a major sub-Arctic facility, named the HAARP Research Station, on an Air Force–owned site near Gakona Alaska".

That is the 'official' version of what HAARP is – from that wonderful font of 'reliable and trustworthy' information (sarcasm again) - highly controlled and suppressed - Wikipedia. So you can relax now and let good old Wikipedia confirm your belief system (they must know more than me)...except, just a minute....critical thinking, for a second or two...? The American military (Black Ops) have spent $Billions on building a highly 'secretive' (did you know anything about it?) installation in the middle of the Arctic in Alaska to *"analyse the ionosphere and investigate the potential for developing ionospheric enhancement technology for radio communications and surveillance"* (hahaha) Oh come on, pull the other one it's got bells on it. If that's all it is, a little research station for studying radio communications, it could have been conveniently built on a Collage campus in the USA, for all to see and benefit from, without the logistical nightmare and expense of having to move all the building materials and technologies to the middle of frozen nowhere. Surely it does not take too much critical thinking to figure that story does not quite add up. Make a search on Youtube – 'The Truth about HAARP' if you need more convincing.

HAARP in Alaska is the largest ionospheric heater in the world capable of heating a 1000 square kilometre area of the ionosphere to over 50,000 degrees. It also has what is known as a 'phased array' - which means the Radio waves it produces are steer-able and those waves can be directed to a selected target area with great accuracy. By beaming radio frequency energy up and focusing it, as they do with this facility, they can cause a heating effect that literally 'lifts' all of the ionosphere within a 30 mile diameter area, which results in changes in localized pressure systems and even the route of jet streams. These Radio Waves, controlled by the U.S. Military (not a civilian 'communications research' company note) are used to create weather events and also they are strong enough to cause earthquakes - and they do.

Harnessed to the insidious Chemtrails, which, due to the heavy metal content in them can amplify and reflect the radio wave energy put out by the HAARP facility, creating a highly accurate and target-able weapon of mass destruction. This 'weapon' has been used many, many times – in fact so often that it is getting easy to tell if a significant weather event is natural or HAARP made. There are detectable specific heat signatures and other tell-tale vibrations and signs that always occur *before* a HAARP triggered event happens, which do not happen during a natural event. The energy from the HAARP created radio waves is tremendous and can have awesome effects. The devastation of the Twin Towers (they were literally turned to dust) was a result of HAARP directed energy. HAARP directed energy also accounts for many extreme weather phenomenon – 'Hurricane Katrina' was HAARP induced, as was 'Hurricane Sandy' and many other recent devastating Hurricanes and floods. HAARP can be used to create droughts like the one in California in 2014 -2015, and snow-storms and all kinds of extreme weather and it has been used against many countries – to relieve them of their natural resources or to help to persuade them to 'toe the 'Globalist'-line. Comply with instructions towards the creation of a 'New World Order'. For example in 2011 Thailand began aligning themselves more with the pro-Russian Southern Asia alliance and away from the heavy influence of the USA and the Globalists, and soon after Thailand suffered some of the most severe floods in their history...Ah, surely just a coincidence...do you think? The south of England also suffered extreme flooding in 2012, this resulted in many private farmers going bankrupt as their fields were turned to useless quagmires. Later to be bought (on the cheap) by Elite owned corporations...hmm, just another unfortunate coincidence...?

The earthquake that destroyed huge parts of Haiti in 2010 was HAARP made. Haiti just happens to be one of the richest countries on the planet, in terms of natural resources. But one of the poorest in terms of their population, most of whom live in abject poverty. The earthquake gave the American government ('puppets' of the Elite ruling Royal and Zionist Jewish Cabal) chance to 'invade' Haiti in order to give them 'aid' of course. But while they were there they made sure that Haiti's natural resources – oil, copper, gold, uranium etc. became under the control of the Archon/Demon 'Elite's' corporations. Many of the earthquakes that have destroyed huge areas of different countries have been HAARP made, for various reasons, but all have had the effect of warning not to cross the ruling Cabal.

The Tsunami that hit Indonesia and Thailand and other countries around the Indian Ocean in 2004 was very likely to have been HAARP created...or perhaps caused by a controlled nuclear explosion. Whatever method was used it was definitely purposely induced and not a natural incident. It was done for many various reasons (too many to go into now) but basically it, again, gave an excuse for an American 'invasion' of Indonesia (to 'give aid' *again*) and while they were there they had a major influence on the Indonesian (Muslim) government becoming more compliant, shall we say, with the 'New World Order' program.

The earthquake that caused the Tsunami that hit Japan in 2011 and (supposedly) caused the disaster at the Fukushima nuclear power plant was also HAARP triggered. (There is some evidence that a nuclear bomb was planted first and this was triggered by HAARP waves). Actually the Tsunami was created as a very convenient 'natural' catastrophe that disguised the deliberate blowing up of the nuclear reactors, which caused, and is still causing, unfathomable amounts of nuclear waste contaminating the atmosphere and the Pacific Ocean. Of course you have not been told, but it has been estimated that the amount of radio-active pollution, so far (and it is continuing *every* day) is enough for this disaster to be considered as a life extinction event. It will certainly eventually cause the extinction of most of the sea life in the Pacific Ocean, and the now virulent radio-active laden atmosphere will, in time, create a massive step towards the 'Elite's' Population culling goal. Already the (unreported – in the mainstream) deaths and cancers and birth defects being caused among the Japanese population is reaching increasingly significant proportions. Search 'Leuren Moret – HAARP-Chemtrials" on Youtube for the full details (and evidence) of all this.

The Demon/Reptilian races cannot survive for long in the Earth's atmosphere as it is/was and they have to be content with controlling their 'human/hybrid puppets' from the confines of another (close) dimension. A monumental shift in the composition of the Earth's atmosphere, as caused by this Nuclear 'accident', and many unreported others, will go a long way towards making the Earth's atmosphere more conducive for them (but deadly for Humans) for more frequent and longer visits...Oh, God help us...and He *will* in ways that I will describe later. 'He'/God being the Source of all Creation/Energy, the God inside us all, not the imaginary fearsome biblical God on a cloud somewhere - or whatever you believe. He would be just as likely to blame the evil of mankind and chuck a thunderbolt at us, as rescue us, from what I can gather from some Old Testament 'religious' stories!

There are many HAARP stations scattered about the world and they are regularly used for all sorts of destructive energy manipulation. It is not the operators at these facilities who are evil – the co-operation of many of them are due to ignorance, mind-control or black-mail. The world controlling Cabal use the colossal HARRP created energy as a weapon against humanity, to force compliance with their 'New World Order' agenda, and as a means of transferring more wealth (power and control) to themselves, and as a tool to create conditions of fear and misery (food for the Demons). The unlimited HAARP energy *could* be used for the benefit of mankind to create free energy, or to create rainfall to turn arid deserts into fertile pastures, or to alter landscapes to divert water, or to find natural resources and minerals deep underground, but, unfortunately, at the moment, as with so many things, evil influences are in total charge of this technology.

Those who are crazy enough to think that they can change the world. . . . do!

21

The Pharmaceutical Industry

Despite all the combined efforts of all the previously
mentioned industries and US military (*all* owned or controlled
by the same mega rich Zionist families) by far the biggest
contributor to the destruction of human health around the
world is the pharmaceutical and the pharmaceutical owned
medical industry. The magnitude of the deception of the
medical profession is just completely and immorally off the
scale. There is not one chemical drug manufactured that can
cure anything, and, on the other hand, there is not one illness
or disease that cannot be *cured* naturally. Nature and Spirit
has provided everything to ensure the life-long health of the
Human Being. If we had been left alone to our own natural
unhindered micro evolution (evolution within species) the
normal – and expected life span of the human body would
be 100 – 130 years, perhaps even longer. The pernicious
influence of the Demons has put paid to that. Of course you
cannot slap a patent on a naturally growing plant or weed,
so no profit to be had there. So anyone who claims they can
cure people with a herb or natural compound is mocked and
ridiculed by the (bought-and-paid-for) mainstream press
(propaganda) and the corrupt-to- the-core medical industry,

as just a total nutter, a quack! And, unfortunately, the easily manipulated and highly gullible public go along with this.

The Rockefeller conceived and owned medical profession is basically an off-shoot of their chemical (oil-based) pharmaceutical corporations, a sales outlet, if you will, for their synthetic and dubious, but *very* profitable, drugs. Okay I accept some chemical drugs *do* have a benefit, I myself have to take 'Warfarin' anti-coagulant tablets to 'thin' my blood because I have an artificial aortic valve, which had installed in my fifties due to an early childhood disease that damaged my natural valve. I often wonder if my immune system had not been compromised by childhood vaccines if this would have happened. Unfortunately for my overall heath I have yet to find a natural alternative to Warfarin (rat poison). As I said some drugs can have a 'beneficial' *effect in* that they relieve and disguise the symptoms of a malady, thus allowing the body to heal itself without the added stress of pain and discomfort. But no chemical drug can actually *cure* anything itself...and most have so many long-term health destroying side-effects, which are actually far more dangerous than the condition they are supposed to be treating.

When I talk about the medical profession in derogatory terms, I am not including trauma doctors and surgeons, who do a wonderful job helping to keep people alive after injury, or disease – just the trained ('programmed') drug-pusher MDs who cause *more* death and suffering world-wide than almost any other cause-of-death. I am not suggesting *every* MD does this deliberately, many believe they are doing good due to their 'programming' – Rockefeller controlled Medical School training, but never-the-less, like it or not, they are all ultimately killers. And of course there are some medical doctors who know full well all about the adverse, and often deadly, effects of the drugs they regularly prescribe, but money and profit are far more crucial to them than the health of people. Read - "**Dead Doctors Don't Lie**" by Dr. Joel Wallach or watch his many presentations on youtube for as much information as you want on this subject.

The Cancer industry (it *is* a for-profit industry) is a prime example of the evil disdain that the (Archon controlled) medical profession has for Human life. Knowing what I do now I get very upset when I see all the well-meaning, but totally misguided events being held 'to fight cancer', for 'cancer research'. The world renowned *annual* 'Terry Fox Run' in aid of cancer research, for example, just one of hundreds of thousands of similar events, has been going for more than 40 years and has reportedly raised $650 million since then for 'cancer research'. Now, come on – critical thinking again...40 years and $650.000,000.00 (and this is only one of countless thousands of similar fund-raisers) and they are still no nearer to finding a proper cure for cancer?... oh, pleeeeease be real. What a joke - surely you can see that? Currently the official cancer *cure* rate is somewhere around 2.5%. It is considered a 'cure' if you survive for 4 years after the (totally barbaric) conventional medical treatments – Chemotherapy, which kills all cells - healthy ones as well as cancerous ones, radiation, which actually causes even more cancer, or surgery, which is always life debilitating.

In actual fact there are dozens of completely natural and virtually 100% effective cures for cancer already known and proven, and the money raised for 'cancer research' is actually used to suppress and renounce these cures. So when you run 'for cancer research' you are, in actual fact, using your time and energy to kill more people. A very sad but true state of affairs. Think about it, just for a moment, what happens to the 'cancer industry' - all the hospitals and doctors and nurses and drug companies and support staff who make a good living from cancer, if the knowledge of *free* cancer-curing, naturally growing plants and herbs and fruits and compounds is made widely available. Of course they *cannot* allow this to happen for monetary (profit) reasons as well as the fact that cancer is one of their greatest assets in the culling of the population.

Cancer is *not* a deadly disease (or shouldn't be). Cancer cells are actually a body defense mechanism against other infections and maladies, which goes out of control. This has to do with many different outside influences – stress, pollution, an undermined (by disease and pharmaceutical drugs – and vaccines) immune system, toxic food and cigarettes and many other deliberately introduced environmental factors. The Cancer Industry concentrate only on trying to treat and control the cancer cells – instead of looking at the underlying causes and reasons for the development of cancer cells in the first place. Cancer is actually a fungus, not a disease and can often be cured by simply oxygenating the blood using a Hydrogen Peroxide protocol, or by drinking Sodium Bicarbonate (simple, and cheap, baking soda) which alkalises the body. Cancer cells cannot live in oxygenated or alkaline conditions. Chemotherapy chemical drugs also kill cancer cells (not very efficiently though and you need lots of the drugs – goody more profits) but, they also kill healthy immune system cells at the same time!

It is a grim and dispiriting mentation I know to think that profit, and power and control, is far more important, to too many 'people', than the well-being of fellow Human Beings. It *is* hard to believe that anyone (*anything*) could have such a malefic mind-set to consider Human life to be so valueless in preference to money (power and control). But, remember the 'people'/entities who are responsible for all this totally lack empathy – they do not think or act in any way remotely similar to a human Human Being.

**Reality is merely an illusion –
albeit a very persistent one.**

111

22
Paedophilia

Unless you have been living in a cave for the past few years, you must have heard, at least, part of the long-running saga of Jimmy Saville and his connection to paedophilia – and his other unsavoury perversions. Then for a period of time it seemed that virtually every celebrity of a certain age was being similarly accused. Of course this mainstream media reporting (as usual) was just a deflection away from the real truth behind the astounding worldwide contagion that is paedophilia. The amount of children that go 'missing' every year (in all countries of the world) is truly staggering. A few of these missing-child cases are publicised to make it look as if the establishment cares and make it seem as if the problem is not really that significant, heart-breaking as it is for the parents. Most of these young children that go missing – and there are hundreds of thousands of them each year worldwide, are lured away or kidnapped to become part of an International baby and child trade, that supplies the rich and (in)famous with sex 'playthings' and subjects for human sacrifices. I absolutely kid you not. This appalling, sick-making...(there are not sufficient evil words to describe it) human trade *IS* happening. Even I, with my open-mind and capability of dealing with most things, found this information hard to swallow – I gagged profusely!

A few isolated cases of sick-minded individual paedophiles, as we are lead to believe, it is *NOT!* Of course, when you know the capacity for limitless evil and horror the Archons/Demons are capable of imbuing their hosts and puppets with, it is actually not so hard to understand and believe. As you have just read the UK Queen and members of the Royal family are partial to a Human baby sacrifice or two (or many!) as is the Pope. (I am sorry, I have trivialised this repugnance with that glib sentence).

Many people cannot understand how Jimmy Saville, at the time, an ageing (slimy) ex DJ and children's 'entertainer' (ugh) could become so friendly with the Royal family of Britain. Indeed he eventually became a part of their 'inner circle'. Recent revelations have answered their queries. Jimmy Saville died a very rich man, with a wealth certainly not commensurate with his C grade ex celebrity status. He was paid handsomely (and the rest) and protected (while he was alive) from all investigation into his own insatiable appetite for sex with children, by the Queen, for his services in providing her with suitable children for her Satanic human sacrifice rituals. And by the government, in particular Prime Minister, at the time, Ted Heath – who was an Olympian child abuser and murderer. This *really* is true I'm afraid, belief system overload or not!

If only, these despicable hybrid humans were the only ones involved, but paedophilia is also absolutely rampant among the politicians in Britain and USA and in most countries around the world. A nice entertaining weekend for some leading politicians and mega-rich business men, involves 'buying' a few young children and setting them free, naked, in a forest, and then hunting them down for 'sport' (like a fox hunt I guess, with sex). Naturally the children are eventually killed...cannot have any 'witnesses' left alive of course. I know, I know, this is yet another thing your 3D mind will not allow you to accept, so call me a 'mentally deranged crank' for writing it. Heck, I must be if I made this up! - But I assure you I haven't (I *wish* I had).

The question is why is there so much paedophilia going on in the world? Why are so many (so-called) leaders in the world partaking in this heinous evildoing? Low vibration emotion such as abject fear and horror is nectar, food, energy to Archontic/Demonic Beings. The energy vibrations from young children below the age of puberty, is particularly 'energising' for these creatures. So not only do they satisfy their perverted sexual/domination urges on young children, they also gorge on the fear and terror (low vibrational energy) of their ill-fated victims. Babies, in particular are seen as little bundles of pure dense 'energy'. I am shaking my head myself in disbelief as I write this, and perhaps this is a step too far for anyone to have to even contemplate, but unfortunately this *is* a part of 3D life on this planet. Further (very) convincing details of this beyond evil paedophilia can be found in '**The Perception Deception**' and in other books by David Icke.

This fiendish demonic evil is not the main subject of this book and I do not wish to labour the point here. Suffice to say that most of the Satanic secret societies that the 'Elite' (wrong use of the word really) controllers of the world, the hybrid Reptilian Humans, belong to, are linked closely to paedophilia. Surely you have heard of ancients sacrificing virgins to appease (various) gods and such like. These human sacrifices are not myths and they certainly did not fade out in modern times – the practice is as rife today as it has ever been. The Roman Catholic church is always being connected with child abuse, especially of little boys (this is widely reported even in the mainstream news) well, you can be assured that the main-stream news reporting is not even denting the very tip on the iceberg of what is really going on in this bastion of *religious(?)* piety. Why is it that little boys are (and they are) more popular amongst the demonic possessed paedophiles? This has to do with accessing the lower chakra at the base of the spine and anal sex does this and triggers nerve vibrations in the victims minds causing severe mental reactions and vibrations, (ho ho the Archons love this) and often leads to the victim's brain suppressing, and later going into self-denial, that the attacks took place, leading often to severe long-term mental damage...easier to control for the future!

There really is no limit to the evilness going on around the globe right under our noses, but this child/baby paedophilia and torture, and sacrifice, surely has to be the most heinous manifestation of it. And this is why we *have* to 'wake up' and together work to stop this hellish evil

When every one is thinking alike, then somebody isn't thinking

23

How bad can it get?

I want to live in a world where all the food is not being systematically poisoned. Where pure clean water is available everywhere. An interesting (I think) aside here – it has been scientifically calculated that there was nowhere near enough *naturally* occurring salt to have caused all the seas and oceans on Earth to have become as saline as they are. And there is speculation (that I personally believe) that the seas and oceans (just energy remember) were deliberately salted by Demonic influenced ETs, to reduce the fresh water on Earth. Control of the water is the control of life.

I want to live in a world where there are no wars and mindless killing just for gain. Where the atmosphere is not being constantly polluted and radiated. Where doctors actually *care* about preserving health and are taught how to do it properly, naturally. Where 'life' (all life) is considered precious above all other things. In a clean, safe and bountiful world without avarice and greed and the need to control. In a world full of love and appreciation for everything in it – in short – in a world without the despicable, evil, demonic, pernicious influences of the Demiurge (Satan) worshipping, Archon/Demon controlled, Reptilians and their empathy lacking hybrid-human puppets.

Of course I am not alone in this – every *human* Human surely would want the same thing, so why can it not be? There are a tiny, tiny few 'people' (Demon/Reptilian puppet/humans) in positions of self-induced power that totally dominate and control everything on the planet, and there are more than 7 billion Humans on Earth, who, given any choice, would rebel against these 'controllers' in an instant. So why hasn't it happened? Of course, because of ignorance and mind-control. The vast majority of Humans have no idea what is really going on in the world, they have no clue that they are slaves that they are so under-the-thumb of hybrid/human masters. They know (most of them) that the world is totally shite but they have no clue that they hold the power to change their lives and the *whole* world for the better. They are just going merrily (I doubt that) about their own little existence, waiting for the next problem they have to face, or for the next episode of "Walking Dead" (how ironic) to watch. It is not their fault (not your fault) that they (and you?) are totally ignorant of the real state of affairs in the world. They, (like you?) just accept that what they (you) see is all there is. "Life is shit then you die" is just the way it is for most people. There is nothing that can be done to counter all the 'crap' in the world. But there *is* a lot we can do, just by being 'awake' – realising and recognising, and accepting, that we *are* being controlled, will make a *dramatic* contribution towards the solution, the annihilation of the Demonic influence. They cannot do anything to stop you 'waking up', and they cannot have any power over you, when you know what they are doing.

As powerful as the Demons and their Earthly puppets are, they would be no match for the combined force of the

Human Race working together in harmony against them. But until this happens – and it will eventually, we have to get through the next few years as best we can. The problem is that before things on Earth get better they are going to get, a lot, worse. As the Demon/Archon's race towards total control of the planet and the "New World Order" and the reduction of the population (Agenda 21) is gaining ever faster momentum. There will be no let-up in the amount of death and destruction causing (manufactured) 'Terrorist' wars being fought around the Globe. Regardless of well-meaning but totally futile rallies and protest marches. There will be no up-turn in the economy, no end to all the 'austerity' programs that are in force in most countries, there will only be ever more debt. There will be no let-up in the amount of airliners going 'missing' and other 'false flag' events such as the (fake) Paris Killings etc. There will be ever accelerative intrusive *security* (ha) surveillance and ever increasing fines for whatever idiotic offence 'the ruling Elite' decide to enforce as a further means of control and wealth transference.

Another interesting aside here – did you know that USA has the largest population of prisoners in the world per capita, *and* in total? Is this because America is the most dangerous and crime-ridden country in the world? No, not by a long way, a huge proportion of these 'felons' in jail are there for pathetic, minor offences, such as non-payment of tax and filling in tax returns wrongly, not paying farcical traffic fines and such like, for publicly giving food to the poor (I kid you not!) It is also interesting to note that American prisoners are forced to work for no, or very derisory, pay and the goods and products they make are sold on the market at normal prices, gaining fantastic profits for the ever-growing (private) prison 'industry'. The more prisoners the more profits for them. Most prisons in the USA can easily offer lower prices on tender than any legitimate manufacturer, even those that employ immigrants on slave-labour rates.

The transfer of wealth from the already poor to the already mega-rich will continue, at an even faster rate giving them even greater wealth (power and control). There are plans for another currency collapse, perhaps even greater than the one in 2008 when the money 'bail-outs' paid by their own puppet governments of the world (Taxes, paid by you and me) to the *private,* Rothschild owned banks (who caused the crash!) were just mind-blowingly obscene.

The 'New World Order' is a single government, unelected of course, with a single digital currency (no cash) a single (enforced) 'religion', a single army and a single law enforcement agency to rule (dominate) the whole world. The idea of a digital currency may at first seem a good one. You have a micro-chip (already being trialed and developed – and used) injected into your arm or wrist and for *everything* you buy your arm is simply scanned – like a debit card is scanned at a store, and the payment is debited from your account. Great, no money to get stolen, no card to lose etc. a good idea. Whoa, wait a minute, the *only* way you can buy anything, including food, is by an electrical signal controlled by the 'bank' (the ruling class who own all the banks). If you do anything to 'step-out-of-line', no matter how minor, that signal can be very easily switched off. Then you have no means at all to buy your water or your food... micro-chip, yes, a great idea - for even more control over the, by then, heavily reduced population.

In this 'New World Order', if it ever came about (we can - and *will* stop it) there would be just two classes of people – the mega-rich Elite few living in a 'Disney World' Utopia with armed (likely Robots – or at least 'Robotic' mind-controlled) 'people' to safe-guard them, and the ultra-poor, you and me, living in little more than high-rise ghettos with everything in life being highly controlled and restricted. Just like the life projected in the movie 'Hunger Games'. This movie, like a great many Hollywood (Jewish) movies, has elements of prediction in it. The mainly Jewish writers and producers of this movie (and others) are 'insiders' - part of the Elite ruling cabal. The rich exclusive cities and the contrasting highly controlled relatively poor 'districts' portrayed in the movie, are depictions of the ultimate goals of Agenda 21/ Agenda 2030.

For evil to thrive it takes good men to do nothing

24

Is Anything 'Real'?

Is anything real? Of course this depends on your viewpoint of reality. If 'real' to you is the limited 3D manipulated and dominated world that you react with on a day-to-day basis, then no, there is certainly not much that is 'real'. Things might appear to be real but that is just testament to how well you have been deceived. Let's take the mainstream news for example...You would be absolutely amazed, horrified, repulsed if you knew just how many world 'events' are faked or deliberately created, to influence public opinion or perception and then earnestly reported as 'terrorist' plots or the acts of 'madmen'. *Most* main newsworthy events are usually cases of 'false-flag' problem-reaction-solution plots to manipulate the 'sheeple' (sheep-like people who can only 'group-think' and unquestionably accept anything they are told by 'authorities') into believing the world is too dangerous for the public and they all need 'protecting' (controlling) by their 'government'. Unfortunately the controlled 'puppets' in government are not interested at all in your safety (they *are* the 'terrorists', the very ones who are making the world ever more unsafe!) they are simply tirelessly working towards your further subjugation.

Virtually all of the so-called 'mass-shootings' widely reported in the 'news' are actually planned and perpetrated by puppet agencies of the ruling Cabal – (CIA MI6 and Mossad usually) who either use mind-controlled 'madmen' dupes to conveniently take the blame for their own professional killers who do the job – or totally fake everything, using actors and theatrical blood and props. The so-called Sandy Hook shootings in a school in America some years ago was an example of totally faked propaganda. Of course it is easy to see why these bogus - or false-flag 'shootings' are carried out, because immediately after all such events the media and government spokespeople cry out for more 'gun control'. The idea is to disarm the public of America, and other countries, of their guns, while at the same time vastly increasing the fierce-some quantity of the weapons and ammunition supplied to police Of course the reason for this is because it is far easier to impose (the planned) military/police control over an unarmed public. This is just another blatantly obvious (to people who are 'awake' enough to see it) step towards the imposition of the 'New World Order'. It really does not matter if innocent people have to be killed (or suckered) in the Byzantine and evil process to achieve this goal.

The so-called 'Charlie Hebdo' shootings in Paris in 2015 were totally faked. France was showing some sympathy towards Palestine's claims to be recognised as an independent sovereign state and so the Zionist Jews had to put a stop to that. The 'shootings' by alleged Muslim 'terrorists' (but staged by Mossad - Israel's secret service agents) created an outcry against Arab Muslims and all thoughts of (Arab Muslim) Palestine were forgotten - job done! The (faked) shootings, in the face of hysterical media coverage also had the advantage of manufacturing further conditions for the introduction of even more draconian 'security' (control) measures.

To me the Nightly or Daily News is akin to watching 'Jackanory' (which was a children's fictional story-time TV program back in the 1960s) and is simply not worth bothering with – it really is just an insult to intelligence. And a comic book has more intellectual integrity than most newspapers. The News, in whatever form, is simply mind-control propaganda designed to alter your perception of life and the world you live in. The threat from ISIS is another example of a fabricated 'terrorist' group (really made up of paid mercenaries organised, trained and financed by the governments and agents of Israel, Britain, the USA and Saudi Arabia) to create conditions of fear for the imposition of even more 'security and liberty-taking, intrusive surveillance – and as an excuse for making war on, and debilitating, countries such as Syria, Libya and Iraq and Iran for geopolitical reasons. The publicised 'be-headings' by these 'fanatical' people were all totally (and comically) faked to elicit obvious and predicted outrage and fear, and demands for action by the dumbed-down news-watching 'sheeple'.

Of course I have some sympathy with people when I hear them earnestly discussing and debating, with bewildering nescience, news-reported current events, but I also despair that they are so blind to the conspiracy to manipulate and mind-control them going on around them. It really is not too difficult to see all the news for what it is - distorted and deliberately misrepresented (propaganda). When some major headline-worthy event happens, that however vaguely, doesn't quite ring true with you (surely most of them?) do some critical thinking, if you haven't already been dumbed-down too much to do that, and carry out some research of your own. Surely you don't want to just be totally taken for a mindless chump (which the Cabal are relying on you being for your compliance, to further their control agenda) and remain in moronic ignorance of the truth behind all the potential life-changing events that seemingly happen with ever more accelerating expediency? Go to '**tomatobubble. com**' for the alternate (true) versions of news events - or search Youtube 'the truth about...' after a few days of the event happening (virtually *every* event). Please, for your sake, as well as mine, and everyone else's (the more people 'awake' the better for everyone) do not just blithely accept what you are told by mainstream sources, which are owned, bought-and-paid-for, by the ruling Jewish Elite. Your future and the future of your family depends upon you 'waking up' and realising what is going on around you, and all the despicable and contemptuous lies and deceit that are being continuously fed to you in an attempt to control your thinking and perceptions and bring about your meek and compliant acceptance of further control and domination.

I know you are probably thinking right now...'Oh, he's one of those deluded people who sees 'conspiracy' in *everything*...Well, yes I do – I see conspiracy in (virtually) everything because it *is* there. Propaganda is one of the biggest weapons that can be used against a population to make them conform and be pliable when planning a major world changing event. The cause of the USA/Vietnam war, for example, has been admitted *in public* – it was brought about by a 'false-flag' event. The attacking of US War ships in the Tonkin bay were not carried out by the North Vietnamese, who were blamed for it at the time, they were carried out by agents of the American (Demon's puppet) government as an excuse to declare war on, and invade, Vietnam. There were many reasons for the Vietnam War (one of the most pointless and evil wars in history) but fighting 'Communism' was *not* one of them. See "Robert Welch explains the purpose of the Vietnam war" on Youtube. The 'News', in the hands of the ruling Elite is little more than blatant and manipulative propaganda and is hardly ever the 'real' truth.

Intuition comes very close to clairvoyance;
it appears to be the extrasensory
perception of reality

25

Perception of Reality

Perhaps you have seen – or, at least, heard of people who can walk over burning coals without pain or injury. How is this possible – is it a trick? No, it's not a trick and people can be 'mind-trained' to be able to do it themselves. Everything we experience in life is down to our perception of what is real and what is reality. As Quantum Physics is proving more each day, *everything* in existence is made up of a form of energetic process - and how this energetic phenomenon is perceived can be different in different people. Fire and flame to most people is hot and harmful, but if the perception of fire can be altered – and with some people (involving trance, meditation, spiritual awareness, self-hypnosis, focus etc.) it *can* be, then fire can be reduced to a harmless percept and present no problem to walk on.

Every Human Being is theoretically able to alter their perception to such an extent as to render potentially pernicious phenomena as harmless – deadly diseases, fire (as the example) even physical trauma. The frantic and desperate mother being able to summon super human strength to lift a massive and heavy object off her child is an example of this altered perception of what is conceived as 'real'. Unfortunately, due to the influence of the Demons/ Archons, which has manifested itself as a false and very limiting viewpoint of ourselves – we *think* I couldn't walk on hot coals, I couldn't lift that weight...I can't – so in 'normal' circumstances, we certainly can't! However if we had been left to our natural state of being, "I can't" becomes a redundant term, because we Humans are ultimately capable of *anything* – of all possibilities.

Travelling through time and space (through 'energetic portals') is not only possible, it has been done including "beam me up Scotty" type travel to Mars (which incidentally is inhabited by several races of ET Beings and has a human military base there) and to other planets. Oh no, here he goes again with the twaddle... "Beam me up Scotty" is pure science fiction and physics would deem it impossible - how can a body be 'dissolved' and then returned to its original state in a new location? Ah, but if you take into account the *true* nature of reality and if you understand that *everything* is just a form of 'energy,' which it is (including the Human body) energy can be altered – rendered into a different state, and then returned to its original state. The "beam me up Scotty" technology in Star Trek is based on scientific *fact* (not fiction) and the technology exists today. "Project Pegasus" is the name of a top secret operation that involves high technological travel in space. And who told you about Martians and other ETs living on Mars, what a laugh – you probably also believe in little 'green men' on the moon? Well, yes – not necessarily by 'little green men' but the moon is inhabited as well.

Man has been going to the moon (thanks to Alien technology) long before the ridiculously fake televised Lunar

Landings of the sixties – which incidentally were produced and filmed by Stanley Kubric. Of course the controlling Elite did not want the public to know about the advanced space travel and anti-gravity energy technology they had, so they created the 'Moon Landings' films. I could write another book about this hoax, but suffice to say here, there is no way that the (supposed power-of-a-calculator technology) space vehicles that they used would get anywhere near the moon – and back! – at the '*first*' attempt! Some more critical thinking here; Would anyone (unless they were totally certain of the outcome) televise to the whole watching world an operation that had never been done before (supposedly) and should have been fraught with unknown risks, without secret trial and error attempts before hand? Which clearly did not happen, otherwise they would have been shown after the apparent successful moon landing. Think about it please – The risks to future financing if the first moon landing failed were simply not worth taking in full public view. The untold $billions subsequently spent by NASA on the 'space program' were totally reliant on nothing but total success – which was provided by the studio created and filmed televised versions.

There are (and have been for a long-time) Human military bases on the moon, and in actual fact the moon is not a natural planet – it is an ancient construct…(!?) read **"Who Built The Moon"** by Christopher Knight and Alan Butler for more details. David Icke in his book "**The Perception Deception**" also explains the purpose of, and reason for, the moon. Yes, yes, I know I am *really* stretching your belief system here, but on what basis would contradict me - your knowledge gained from the (highly controlled) mainstream media and group-think, the accepted 'norm', or your (false) 'education'? Have you ever stopped to think that there may be a reason that you are *expected* to simply laugh and disbelieve any alternate premise to your mind-manipulated belief system. Indeed you have been taught and brought up and pressurised to act this way – it is highly necessary for the continued control that the ruling Cabal have over us. If too many people start to question all the (bogus) knowledge they are continually feed by (often) well-meaning but misinformed teachers, scientists and news reporters, the control the Cabal has over us will start to crumble. So you may laugh and pour scorn on me and think of me as an idiot ("ah, he's just crazy") but, think about it, who is the *real* idiot? Ah, at least my 'idiocy' is based on deep research, interest, and critical thinking, and a (thankfully) open-mind! As I have already assured you there is so much more to 'reality' than you have been lead (and fed) to believe.

In the 'reality' that we Humans were *meant to* experience, war would be totally purposeless because nobody would perceive of being killed or injured, so they couldn't be. Corruption would be pointless, because no one would perceive of being deceived, so they couldn't be, and so on. Even 'physical' objects that we interact with could be perceived as not harmful, and banging into a shower door would not be perceived as painful or damaging – so it wouldn't be. The only states of being would be unconditional love, inner peace and empathy – no pain, or fear, or disease or physical damage would be perceived. This is what the true destiny of the Human Race was meant to be and one day will be!... in a higher dimension than our current lowly and dense 3D world.

Even if we had been left alone in our development as a species and we became as enlightened as we were *meant* to be 'death' would still be an inevitable part of the 'cycle of life'. The body - 'body/computer vehicle' for our 'Consciousness' (some might call it the 'Soul') would still eventually deteriorate and stop, but at a much older age. But, the concept of death, as we currently understand it, is totally wrong. We, our Consciousness (Soul) *never* dies – it is eternal and is 'recycled' over and over again. We have *all* lived many times before, possibly on a different planet or in a different universe or dimension. Each time 'life' – a new 'body/computer' vehicle,' is brought into the world (baby born) a new Consciousness/Soul is *not* necessarily produced for it. An existing Soul, recently parted from another 'body/computer vehicle' – or sometimes maybe not recently (I will explain this later...) will take up 'residence' in a new one. Even parts of mainstream science have accepted proof of life after 'death' although perhaps, with their limited (programmed) 3D perception, they don't fully understand it yet. Dr Eben Alexander, a neurosurgeon at Harvard University for 15 years was struck by e-coli meningitis in 2008. His brain basically died. For 7 days he was 'clinically dead' - during this time his 'consciousness' (Soul?/energy) experienced 'life after death'. 'Miraculously' he revived and later he wrote a book **'Proof of Heaven'** about his experience in the 'afterlife'.

Ah, I have a question...yes? ...if no new 'Consciousness' or Souls are created for each new life produced how many Souls were created in the beginning? I mean, there are millions more people on the planet now than there were before. Were there millions of Souls just hanging around waiting for a 'life to be created for them? In effect yes, enough Souls (energy/conciousness) were created in the beginning, but these Souls could have been experiencing 'life' on different planets, or in other dimensions and then they might have 'chosen' to come to this planet, to help with its development in some way. I understand that this may be a difficult concept for you to grasp – but, I assure you I am not just making all this stuff up. There is masses of empirical evidence for all this. Remember there are many ET entities and higher life forms on this planet and regularly visiting it, and interacting with ever more and more people, and this is where a great deal of (previously suppressed) knowledge is coming from. I will also address the query here about an existing Soul not always being 'installed' in another Human body/computer vehicle straight away. As a Soul gains ever more experience through different lives, in different times, and maybe on different planets, it might get to the stage where it is able to access higher dimensions and then may decide to move away from Earth, to return at a later time.

Moving to higher dimensions can only happen when a Soul reaches a high enough vibration which comes from love and trust and empathy and the freedom from fear that true knowledge can bring. All energy causes vibration and *everything* – even inanimate objects like words and symbols have wave-form vibrations. Positive words like Love and Peace have much higher vibrations than negative words like Fear and Hate. This can actually be proved and the work of Japanese researcher Dr. Masaru Emoto and his

Water Crystals experiments graphically shows the incredible differences in the energies of different words. Youtube search **"The Power of the Word: Dr. Masaru Emoto and Water Crystals"**

Remember the only way a human can react with anything in this 3D reality is through the five senses, which rely on electrical signals caused by vibrating wave-forms being decoded in the brain, so is it really any wonder that our perception of the whole of the limitless 'potentials' of reality is so constricted at the moment. Add to that the most powerful weapon the Demon/Reptilian controllers have in ensuring our continued lack of the true perception of reality – the television – and the subjugation of the human race is easy.

It has not been dubbed as 'the boob-tube' for nothing. The TV is, without doubt (anyone want to argue?) the single biggest cause of falling intellect world-wide. The dumbing-down of the population (and the rise of group think) of most countries, has been spectacular since the introduction of television. And surely (?) you must have noticed over recent years that the quality of TV programs are getting ever worse, ever more banal and juvenile - as they cater for an ever increasingly dumbed-down audience. And also the 'news' programs are ever increasing in their time on air. Most 'news' programs are 24 hours now – ever increasing time for mind-manipulating propaganda. And surely (?) you must have noticed, regardless of which channel and which program you watch, all 'news' is virtually the same... doesn't that tell you something? It should tell you that there is a single source (highly controlled) for all major news' and the 'news' reporters just obediently regurgitate whatever they are told to. Not many critical thinkers among news reporters – or if there are, their compliance is easily bought with (enough) money (power and control). As we have seen *most* (major) news is 'manufactured' with the goal of altering the perception of reality.

REALITY IS NOTHING MORE THAN PERCEPTION

26

The Purpose of 'Death'

The seemingly pointless and nugatory 'deaths' of people in wars, or in accidents, or by disease, or by murder etc. are not *pointless* they have happened for a reason – *all* deaths happen for a purpose. If a 'life' (of a body/computer vehicle') is tragically cut short at an early age (or at any age) it is because the particular Soul in residence in the now deceased body was needed elsewhere. As traumatic as this obviously is for parents, relatives, and friends the 'death' of the body/computer vehicle was necessary at that time. There are no coincidences in nature and 'coincidental' events leading up to a seemingly freak accident (or people being 'in the wrong place at the wrong time') causing their demise, are *not* coincidences, and the deaths caused are a part of the 'learning' experiences for those particular Souls, and they move on to another 'life', to another body/computer vehicle (baby) for more experiences. Could this knowledge give a little solace for the relatives and friends of the deceased? Their loved ones are 'reborn' and their 'lives', however short - or long, (however their 'deaths' were caused) served a great purpose in the development of an eternal Soul. Personally I somehow *knew* (remembered?) innately, spiritually, heart knowledge, from an early age that life was more than just a fleeting experience, it had to be, given the complexity of nature and of the body and mind. To me all this makes perfect sense and I can live life with no fear of 'death' – sure this 'life' I am experiencing now will end one day...but then, I (my Consciousness/Soul) will be back again gaining more experience as someone else.

The only negative part of this scenario is that we cannot remember our past lives and therefore cannot relate to them, and hence, when we start again, we have no idea of our past experiences to learn from on a conscious level (subconsciously many people *do* remember their past lives, or at least parts of them). Often this remembering, knowledge, can be retrieved by regressive hypnosis. Under 'normal' circumstances unfortunately as we currently are, the knowledge of our past lives is not readily available to us because of the limitations on our perception and awareness inflicted upon us by the demonic Archons. Given time and a massive change in our (perceived) reality (that is coming) we will all get to a stage, after however many different 'life' experiences we need to get there, where we *will* remember past lives and benefit from the experiences of them.

Many people often get a sense of Deja vu - "I have been here before, I am sure I have, but I have no idea when..." "I remember that person, ah, but I have never met him before I'm sure of it..." Well, indeed you *have* been to that place before, you *have* met that person before and these are fleeting memories coming to you from a previous life. A baby does not *learn* motor skills, or *learn* how to walk, or talk he/she is *remembering* how to do these things. Growing up is a journey of remembrance more often than actually *learning* new things. Of course there will be some things to *learn* that even an 'old' Soul will not have experienced before – and this is the point of 'living' a new life. I know, this all sounds very fanciful and notional and you can make of it what you will, but consider, if you simply dismiss this as ramblings, or the result of my wishful/delusional thinking, you *might* be depriving yourself of invaluable knowledge.

You are never listening to what someone is saying – you are only ever listening to what you are hearing . . .

27
Help is at Hand

I have 'talked' continuously here of the malevolent Demons/
Archons and their demonic influences and control over
other entities, and Humans, on Earth - and rightly so
because they are responsible for the distortion of our planet,
and have been, for many thousands of years. However there
are other 'Higher Beings' and extra-terrestrial entities who
have an interest in the welfare of our planet and everything
on it. These Beings, including 'our relatives' the Beings that
seeded Earth in the first place, have been watching, with
great interest and dismay, the unfolding of our history and
development (distorted development) and the invariable and
incessant devastation of our beautiful planet.

Higher Beings and Intelligent Civilisations throughout
the 'Omniverse' (all the countless Universes and other
dimensions) live or exist by a code known as the 'Prime
Directive' or 'Universal Law'. Part of this 'Prime Directive'
is all intelligent entities should have 'freewill'. There are
many Higher Beings who could and would help us Humans
in our plight with the Demons, but are forbidden to do
so by the Prime Directive. They have to leave us to our
'freewill'. Of course the great majority of Earth's population
actually do *not* realise that they have 'freewill' in this sense

(so insidiously are they controlled). If enough of the people on Earth did 'wake up' and realise that our *whole* reality is so contorted and controlled by evil (surely as each day passes it is getting harder and harder *not* to recognise this?) we could *ask* with our freewill for help from some of the benevolent Beings who have the power to help us against the Demon's evilness.

These benevolent Higher Beings, although not able yet to intervene or interfere directly by stopping and reversing all the Archonic Demons devastating effects on us and our planet, are actually already aiding us in subtle ways. The escaping radiation from nuclear disasters such as Fukushima and Chernobyl and from all the other leaking (unpublicised) nuclear power plants around the world, is being mitigated somewhat by them, and the ever increasing threat of a nuclear World War 3, currently being planned and manipulated into existence by Archon Puppets in the USA, Israel and the UK, is being thwarted. (Youtube search "WW3" will give you the details). There have been very credible reports of 'Aliens' disarming nuclear weapons in the past when they have been on the verge of being used. The atmosphere, destroyed by Chemtrails and HAARP use, is being 'looked after' so it does not become a human life extinction causing toxic mess, or becoming weakened so much to cause a threat to all life on the planet from Solar radiation. Also they are directly interacting with some 'old Souls' (in the form of babies and children, known as Star Children - more about them in a moment) and helping these Star Children to develop to their *full* potential of powers in order for them to, in turn, help with the enlightenment ('waking up') of mankind.

There is currently quite a major space war going on in our Universe, the Archontic entities that are plaguing Earth and other planets, in defiance of the "Prime Directive" are being assailed on many fronts and in many ways in an effort to get rid of these execrable vermin. If enough people on Earth (it will take only a relatively small percent of the world population) were 'awake' and 'knowing' we could *request help* and Earth could be totally cleansed of all Demonic influences in an instant, and all the destruction to the atmosphere and our world countered in a twinkling, and life on this planet would be paradise *again*. Ah, more rubbish…all the problems to the climate and all the toxic pollutants all over Earth reversed in moments? Come off it – it will take thousands, perhaps millions, of years for all the radiation and other damage to the atmosphere and to Earth to be neutralised. Ah, but you are thinking in 3D again, you are forgetting – everything, *everything* in existence is just a form of energy, and energy can be altered in a split second. The time it takes to turn on a light. So please *'wake up!'* for your own sake as well as everyone else's - let's ask for and get all the help we can.

All this information comes from interaction with Alien Beings in the form of direct communication and 'channelling'. A google or Youtube search for **'James Gilliland'** and/or **'Kryon'** will furnish more details.

"A life not examined is a life not worth living"

28

Star Children – Cosmic Humans

There is a race of Beings on this planet right *now* which is ever increasing in number and influence. These Beings are visually indistinguishable from Humans, you would not know they were any different to anyone else just by looks, however they each have many advanced and spectacular attributes and abilities. They are the 'Bringers of Light' (higher vibrations) and they are here to help and guide the 'awakening' of man to higher consciousness and dimension. Often known as Star children, or when they grow older as Cosmic Humans, these Beings are essentially hybrid Alien/Humans. Although born naturally to human parents these children are heavily influenced and manipulated (in a very benevolent way) by Higher Beings from a very early age. Their manipulated and altered DNA has up to ten fold the information of the average human child. Part of their Alien 'upbringing' involves frequent beneficent visits onto Alien craft for learning and spiritual experiences, and to be endowed with extraordinary abilities. These children all have much higher than normal agility and problem solving skills and are usually very creative. They can communicate telepathically, they can also communicate using a totally unique and complicated signing language when they meet each other, as well as the verbal language of their birth and the thought-languages of their Alien benefactors. Many of these children can use various parts of their bodies to see. There have been (recorded) incidents when some of these children have been blind-folded but are still able to read the headlines of a newspaper scanning the page with their bare hands. Another child has been seen to do the same feat, with his feet – still inside his shoes! Ah, phewy, ridiculous! To me, even without the recorded evidence (which, of course could be faked – but why?) it seems perfectly feasible. As I keep reiterating – *everything* in existence is just a form of energy and words on paper have energetic wave forms. The energy of the words can be picked up by ultra-sensitive and trained receptors, such as those in the hands and feet of these extra-human children (and later adults). All Humans, if they had an unadulterated (micro) evolution without the mind-limiting and perception-changing influence of the Demons, would have been able to do all this.

As with all the subjects I have covered in this book there is a great deal of evidence and proof about the existence of these 'super-beings' all over the Internet. Google or Youtube search '**Mary Rodwell, Star children**' for example. Of course the highly controlled mainstream media in most countries will not give any publicity about, or even acknowledge these super Beings. Remember the controllers of the media (and all other aspects of Human life) want/ need you to believe you are just an accident of the cosmos, a meaningless creature with the same origins as a cockroach - to make you easier to control and dominate.

However there are places on Earth that are not so tightly restricted. In Mexico, for instance, the existence of UFOs and ETs and their interactions with Humans is widely known and commonly accepted, indeed they even have TV 'news' programs and documentaries featuring UFO sightings, which they take seriously and do not ridicule or suppress. Star children in Mexico City are monitored and learned from. The Himalayas is another place where many Star Children and Cosmic Humans are widely known about and supported, and in some areas of China Star Children are being fostered and encouraged to use and develop their abilities by the state. Abilities that include; being able to open a flower bud by merely thinking about it, and healing with just the power of positive thought, and being able to change human DNA molecules in a Petri dish (in front of cameras). They are also known there as 'super psychics' due to their very advanced psychic and telepathic abilities.

When interviewed by Mary Rodwell

Mary Rodwell is a professional counsellor, hypnotherapist, ufologist researcher and metaphysician. Mary is the founder and Principal of ACERN (Australian Close Encounter Resource Network) and is recognised Internationally, as one of Australia's leading researchers in the UFO and Contact phenomenon. She is the Vice-President of Star Kids Project Ltd and an Advisory Committee member of Exopolitics.

all these children have similar stories, they have memories of being on space craft and being educated there. They remember their past lives, including ones where they were not Human. They are capable of divulging information that they could not have consciously 'learned'. They feel 'alienated' being on Earth, they know they are different and often they cannot form meaningful relationships with Humans, who many feel are barbaric and primitive. In short these Star Children and Cosmic Humans are exactly what we Humans should have been like by now, and would have been, had we, as a species, been influenced and educated by our benevolent Extra Terrestrial ancestors, instead of the demonic Archons.

You have surely heard about Alien abductions happening over the past thirty – forty years? But in a very limited and most likely disparaging way. "Local Hair-dresser Abducted and Subjected to Weird Sex Experimentation by Aliens" - oh, yeah...right! The stories that do get some mainstream coverage are usually reporting these types of malicious abductions, where bizarre and intrusive experiments are carried out on the abductees, usually by malevolent small 'Grey Beings', which of course most of the public are very sceptical about. I am sure these types of abductions *are* happening all around the world on a regular basis. Indeed there is enough evidence provided by the first-hand accounts of so many different abductees all over the globe (who are total strangers to each other and very unlikely to be 'comparing notes' but who all recount very similar experiences) that prove they happen. However these types of abductions are only a tiny minority of all the interactions with humans and ETs going on around the planet right now, and most are highly advantageous to Human Beings.

As I have already mentioned there are a great many Alien races who are not only benevolent towards Earthlings, but they also have a vested interest in helping with our evolution as a species for many different reasons. Among these reasons are; some are our actual ancestors (family) as a result of them seeding our planet, or of direct intervention with early Humans. Some are empathetic Beings who want all cosmic entities to have the opportunity to develop to their full potential, to make our

Universe (and all Universes) a nicer place. And some simply want the destruction of the evil Demons everywhere they have infected the inhabitants of a world.

The world we live in, past the oh-so-limited 3D perception of most people, is *really* fascinating and exciting and up-lifting. It is a world that makes even the most outrageous 3D science-fiction seem tame and dull. It is a world that actually *does* exist despite most people's inability (programming) to believe it. It is a world of Aliens and Angels and Unicorns and Demons and Reptilian and, countless other, Entities and Beings (most being benevolent to humanity). Of inconceivable 'star gates' and space and time travel, and of natural healing and spiritual awareness. Of endless 'life' and unlimited knowledge. Of unimagined physics and science, and limitless potential for anything that can be dreamed of. And of unconditional love, joy, peace and harmony. All this, and so much more, is yours for the taking...eventually. Just start making the first small steps towards it by 'waking up' and opening your (controlled and programmed) mind. Get yourself in harmony with the increasing higher vibrations of Earth and decrease and restrict the Demon's hold on you - and your evolution to the next level will be assured.

**Life is not about finding
yourself...
Life is about
Creating yourself!**

29
Free Energy

As well as cosmic assistance, which is currently helping to mitigate the worse of the evil excesses of the Demons and their Earthly 'puppets', there are also many Humans who are close to providing the ultimate solution to the Archontic influences. These (independent) scientists and, often amateur, inventors are pursuing the promise of 'zero-point energy'.

Nikola Tesla should be proclaimed as one of the greatest men in the history of the planet, and he surely would have been had his inventions and discoveries been allowed to develop unhindered. Instead this true genius is hardly known about and is hardly mentioned in any mainstream 'History' books. We can thank (blame) a Jewish Archontic 'puppet' called JP Morgan (J P Morgan Bank of the 2008 bank bail-out fame) for this. As an entrepreneur JP Morgan, in the late nineteenth century, had his grubby hands in many 'pies', looking, as ever, for a profit ("my boy"). Amongst these pies, he was financing Tesla's fledgling work in the field of electricity generation. Tesla had discovered a way to harness the energy that makes up the very fabric of space. Consider that Earth has two magnetic poles and spins (quickly) around its own axis in space (which is a ''sea' of massive energy) does this remind you of anything? An electric motor? He was able to produce (and control) electric power from the 'air'. <u>Free</u> energy – unlimited *free* energy that had the potential to supply the whole world, every corner of it, with abundant limitless, clean energy, for every application that can and could ever be thought of. Instead, of this we have the dirty, inefficient and completely corrupt oil/fossil fuel, and the perilous/lethal nuclear power, produced, electricity, that has been a total blight on the whole planet. (Great for the Demons and their obscenely rich Jewish puppets, though!)

Nickola Tesla's electricity needed no wires, it just came direct 'out of the air'. The benefits of this power, energy, for humanity were absolutely prodigious. But unfortunately one Jewish man would benefit himself far more without Tesla's electricity. For a start Tesla's electric power could not be metered, he had light bulbs light up from no visible source. So no profits for JP Morgan there. So his funding for Tesla's work was stopped. And further more JP Morgan's company provided copper wire for the transmission of an alternate source of electric power, produced by spinning a dynamo, powered by an external steam or fossil fueled engine. Very efficient! (*Sarcasm*). But, vastly inferior as this electricity production was, it could be metered and charged for, and the amounts of wire needed for its delivery were astronomical – as were the profits for JP Morgan. To ensure only one (the highly profitable one for JP Morgan) source of electricity was available Tesla's research facilities were destroyed and he was totally discredited as a fraud and a crank (sound familiar?)

Nickola Tesla was not the only inventor to harness 'zero point' energy, free energy from the atmosphere. Many brilliant people have produced and refined zero point energy generators, machines that produce electric power themselves without any external power source – other than the air. Most of these machines have been captured and suppressed and taken away to be stored ingloriously in giant anonymous warehouses, and the inventors beaten and threatened, and discredited. Such is the desperation to keep this technology under wraps while there is still oil and nuclear power to be exploited by the 'Elite' few. To hell with the needs of the population of the world, when there are profits to be made for the Elite Jews (rubbing hands) "my boy".

The problem with inventing a free energy device is that the inventor, quite rightly, wants to become wealthy, immensely wealthy, from the sale of his electricity generators, but, of course, this can never happen. No patent will ever be allowed on such a machine and its production will always be thwarted, by extreme measures if necessary. At this moment in time there are several 'free' energy generators working efficiently and cost free around the world, but these, of course, will never be allowed to be put into mass production. However, there is a consortium of independent scientists and inventors currently working on producing plans for 'home-made' zero-point energy devices. These people will not benefit financially from this work, because the idea is to introduce a blueprint, for a relatively easy-to-make free-energy generator, on the Internet for no or little cost – so that people all over the world can download these designs, before action can be taken by the 'authorities' to suppress or ban them. Once this happens (within the next few years) the whole Archontic Empire will start crashing down around their ears. Without their control over energy the demonic puppet governments and corporations will have no more power (pun intended) over us.

After the end of the ruling Elite cabal, anti-gravity technology, which has existed and has been suppressed since the Second World War, will be made generally available. Imagine the significance of this for mass transportation. Commercial airlines will be using super-fast, noiseless, non-polluting, minimum maintenance, and virtually cost-less flying machines and 'flying saucers' for their services. Personal transport (flying cars) will use the same technology. This is actually what should be happening today, if so much power and control and profit in the hands of a demonic few, had not been inflicted on the planet. Perhaps you think all the flying cars and other craft depicted in many modern Si Fi movies is just an amazing figment of someone's imagination – in fact they are based on already existing technology.

The technology for cars and motorcycles to run on nothing but water also exists *today*. A few modifications to the internal combustion engine and water in the Service Station pumps instead of petrol is all that is required... but where's the profit, and more importantly the control, in that? If you start to just imagine, even a little, how all these suppressed technologies could have and should have, benefited all of mankind, and contributed to the health and well-being of our home planet, surely you must feel anger and resentment at how we have been treated by those 'in charge'. Treated as ants, to work for the money (taxes and debt interest) to keep these vermin in power over us. Actually anger and resentment are negative emotions (the very ones that the Demons feed on) so try not to feel them.

Just, for your sake, and everyone else's sake...*Wake up!* 'Smell the coffee', as they say. Look around you, with *open* eyes, the world has gone to shit in a handcart. Can't you, honestly *see* it? The ruling Elite are counting on it, that you cannot visualise further than the next (obscenely over financed) Premiership match, or infantile video from some totally untalented 'Pop Stars'. 'Gangnam Style'---oh, lord gimme a break!

No one is suggesting that you can go out and totally change the world yourself, but to *see* and *accept* that there *has* to be more to life than you are currently experiencing, is a first step that will inevitably lead to a better future for you - for ALL of us! Continue to enjoy Pop videos and soccer/football matches, whatever, if that helps to make you slightly more content with your life 'experience'/'game', but realise that these are just deliberate distractions to keep your thoughts and focus away from the real issues. In the meantime Archontic influenced puppet politicians and 'World leaders' continue to rape and pillage and wreak havoc around the globe at the behest of the ruling 'Elite' crime cabal. No wonder the world is in such an incredible mess...who put these people in charge? Uh – NO ONE! They made themselves rulers of the world while we were all 'asleep'. Remember it is not incompetence that has led to all the ills of the world – it is *all* by design!

"TO DIFFER IS TO THINK"

30

What can I ('little me') do?

"All this knowledge is very interesting, but how does it affect me in my 'little' life...I am just me, what can I do about it?" Just knowing it (and of course accepting it – or even just a bit of it) will make a *massive* difference to you and everyone else on Earth, even if you do nothing else. Remember we, every single individual, are all 'waves' in the same 'Ocean' and what one person does or thinks *can* have an effect on literally millions of others. Each and every person that 'wakes up' and understands what is really going on, will subtly change the vibration of their energetic field, their aura. We, living beings, (and everything else) are all basically just energy vibrations and we all vibrate at slightly different frequencies at different times. Fear and worry and depression, anger and hate and all other negative emotions will cause us to vibrate at lower frequencies. It is these lower vibrations that 'feed' the Demons. They parasite their energy (food) from the low vibrations of Human Beings in a state of despair and fright.

Let me ask you a question – two questions actually... when you see what is going on all around the world – all the corruption, the rapacity (of the few) and the poverty (of the many). All the endless wars, all the invasive 'security' at airports and other public arenas and all the surveillance cameras everywhere (it has nothing to do with security, just control). The manipulation of the news, which is truly staggering. All the fake events produced, using actors and theatrical effects to exaggerate, or create, public perceptions and induce fear. All the real news, like cures for Cancer being ignored in favour of banal revelations about a celebrity's sex life or whatever (distraction). All the thuggery and crime and racism, all the disease and famine, all the pollution and toxic pesticides and other chemicals tainting food and water. All the worry and anxiety about losing jobs and homes. The mercilessness of the debt economic system endlessly transferring wealth from the poor to the already mega rich. All the mind-numbing 'crap' on TV and hideous (subliminal) advertising. The dumbing-down of education and the infantile rubbish that passes for modern Pop music and Art. All the (manipulated) severe weather events and apparent airplane 'accidents' and 'disappearances' (most are very deliberately planned and executed, for various self-serving interests by the ruling cabal). And all the other endless strife and changes (always for the worse) that are introduced by 'governments' on a daily basis. Don't you ever think enough is enough already, this is not quite right? And don't you ever think of what is really causing it all... can it really all be just 'human nature' and stupidity? Of course not!

Everything is always negative – there is never any positive, feel good, news, apart from maybe a few little local happenings. Now you know the reason for all the doom and gloom – it is all deliberately manufactured, for many reasons, chief among them is control and domination (furthering the agenda of total world control - the 'New World Order') and another is to keep the Demons strong and dominant, they feed off all the negative, low vibrational energy that all these depressing and fearful events and circumstances create in Humans.

On the other hand if you are happy, content, relaxed and loving, your body (body/computer vehicle) and spirit (Soul/Consciousness) vibrates at a much higher level, which is an absolute abhorrence to the Demons. Please 'wake-up' and 'see' and appreciate, that the world *is* in total disarray (surely not that difficult?) and it simply *cannot* be the result of man's folly. Just consider how you think about what's going on and understand that virtually everyone else also thinks the same way. Everything always seems to be changing for the worst. Never ending inflation, higher taxes for this and that, ever increasing prices for electricity, gas and water, for nothing more than further wealth transfer, to increase the already obscene profits for the owners of these utility providers. Cut-backs in public spending, pension funds going 'bankrupt' (being stolen), ever more rules and regulations to follow, higher fines for ever more trivial 'offences", more crime, less efficient police, more moral decadence, uncontrolled immigration, and the unbelievable scourge of childish 'Political Correctness' – is it still legal to call Christmas, Christmas? Ah, our 'elected' leaders – governments, are responsible for the mess due to their rank incompetence. That is patently not possible, all the governments throughout history cannot *all* be incompetent, yet they have *all* furthered the decline of the (micro) evolution of mankind in one way or another. If you can 'wake-up', even if only a little, your 'vibrations' will get higher. The more you 'see' and understand what life and 'reality' *really* is, the less frustrated and fearful and angry you will feel, and the less 'food'/energy for the Demons you will supply. To the ultimate benefit of all of us!

This planet of ours, and all life on it, was originally designed and created to be Utopia and it will be again one day. There is no death, only eternal life for man's Spirit/ Soul/Consciousness. You will come back and experience new things after your current computer/body vehicle stops. The more people knowing this and losing their fear and negative emotions and understanding that this 'life' we are all living at the moment (regardless of whether it is good or bad) is just one tiny 'learning experience' in the great scheme of things, the higher the collective vibrations of the "Ocean" (world population) will be. The higher vibrations of the planet will eventually lead to the inevitable destruction of the Satanic Demiurge (Devil) worshiping Demons and their Reptilian and human/hybrid puppets on Earth who cannot survive without low vibrational energy.

Of course there is no way that the whole population of Earth will 'awaken' and many people, through their dogma and tenet, or more often through a lack of opportunity to be exposed to this knowledge, will be left to their fate in this particular life/experience. Meanwhile, as more and more people *are* seeing the 'light' the future has the ever increasing potential to be brighter sooner. If you know what is really happening to you, the control you are under simply cannot be sustained. Sure, you have to continue to play the 'game' (of life) and try to make the best of it you can, but it will be with a much greater sense of freedom and tranquility and *true* knowledge.

How can you become more intelligent, insightful and truly knowledgeable than the (so-called) brightest scientists, physicists and intellectuals on the planet – overnight?... Simply by 'waking up' and accepting what I am telling you here, while they continue being fooled and duped, or financially blackmailed, by their programmed, left-brained, limited 3D perception of reality.

What screws us up most
in life is the picture in our head of how life is...

31
Pineal Gland

Do you know anything about your Pineal gland? What it is? Where it is? I didn't until just a few years ago and being as this is a major and important organ of the body, I wonder why that is? Why are we not taught about the incredible Pineal gland in biology at school? Because our Pineal gland is our way out of the Demonic control system. From birth onwards the knowledge of this small but marvelous part of the brain is suppressed and neglected and forgotten about, by design.

The Pineal gland is a small organ, shaped a little like a pine cone – hence its name, and is located between the two hemispheres of the brain, in a line between and just slightly above the eyebrows. It is known as the 'third' eye, or 'spiritual antenna'. The great philosopher Plato referred to the Pineal gland as the 'Eye of Wisdom'. There is a lot of myth and conjecture surrounding this pea-sized gland, but basically it can be regarded as our sixth sense. I mentioned earlier that all the wisdom and knowledge of *everything* in Creation exists in the energetic field/matrix that is all around us and the Pineal gland *should* enable us to access all this knowledge with ease.

Now imagine you controlled the World, it is your 'plaything', your personal domain, and you want it exactly the way it suits you (in chaos, anarchy and disarray) and you want total dominion over the population, the last thing you want is a race of 'spiritual', free thinking people able to access all the knowledge of Creation. So, of course you do not want the general public to be aware of this gland, otherwise your plans are scuppered. So you do everything you can to make sure this amazing 'seat of learning' is ignored. In fact you do much more than that you actively, negatively impact its development in any way you can. By introducing fluoride in the water supply for example. Fluoride is also added to most toothpastes, used all over the world, it is a heavy-duty neurotoxin that calcifies the Pineal gland and renders it totally ineffective. Mercury, found in vaccines and in amalgam tooth filings and in Chem-trails, and anywhere else they can put it to ensure its ingestion by the populace, also very efficaciously destroys Pineal gland function.

One of the ways the Pineal gland *should* function is that it is capable (if de-calcified and 'awakened') of producing a chemical called DMT (Dimethyltrytamine). This chemical also naturally occurs in some plants found in the Amazon jungle and is used by native shaman to make a mind-expanding brew called Ayahausca. Drinking Ayahausca enables the person to experience a higher level of being, of consciousness, and to tap into the cosmic knowledge field. Apparently (if done correctly) it is a very profound and life-changing experience (I have yet to have). Your mind basically leaves your body and you enter into a higher vibrational and more spiritual state of existence and catch glimpses of other higher realities and dimensions. No wander the 'controllers'

(Demons) do not want a recognised and fully functional Pineal gland, producing natural DMT, in any of its 'slaves'.

Even a calcified and untrained Pineal gland however provides some elements of a sixth sense, instinctual and higher cognitive processes that can, on occasions, guide your actions.

It is possible to de-calcify the Pineal gland and re-awaken it. Take away all sources of Mercury from your mouth and body; get your amalgam tooth fillings removed. De-detoxifying your body from the ravages of heavy metals, includes a diet of lots of green vegetables (preferably juiced) and organic (where possible) fruits, and supplements such as Spirulina, Wheatgrass and Chlorella, Eat as little cooked food as possible (cooking anything above 120 degrees F kills most of the nutrition in food) NO processed food *at all* and avoid fluoride at all costs. On top of this you will need to practice meditation techniques quite seriously, and train to relax with T'ai Chi and Yoga. A *BIG* lifestyle change for most people, and a lot of effort, but also a lot of 'reward' for doing it.

Some people like living in black and white worlds. Let them stay there! Appreciate all the colours in your world though!

32

The Tide is Turning

December 21st 2012 was widely predicted as being the 'end of the world'. But December 21st 2012 came and went and we are all still here – which proves, I guess, for you doubters, that 'conspiracy theories' *are* just the mad ramblings of 'tinfoil-hat' crackpots. But, wait a moment... it wasn't serous 'conspiracy theorists' (conspiracy 'un-coverers') who predicted this, it was religious zealots and 'New Age' practitioners and their like. Their ideas were based on the cataclysmic predictions of the Mayan Calendar that this particular date heralded as the End of the World. For any serious researchers this, of course, was a total joke. However this Mayan predicted date was highly significant for a totally different reason. Far from it being the end of the world – it was in fact the beginning of the start of a 'new world' – a new era...

According to the Mayan calendar 2012 marked the ending of a five thousand (5125) year astrological cycle and signals a dramatic change for our planet and the people on it. Ancient Theology Astrology expert Santos Bonacci explains that it is part of the Cycle of Precession, which is based on the 24,000 year elliptical orbit of the sun. The sun's 'sister' star Sirius also has a similar orbit and when the Sun and Sirius are the closest they get to each other they enter the sign of 'Aquarius' (remember the popular and optimistic song in the 80s ...'this is the dawning of the age of Aquarius...'?) and a 2000 year "Golden Age" begins. During the Cycle of the Precession the sun takes around 2000 years to pass through each sign of the zodiac and each 'sign' influences Earth, as it does people in different ways, relating to their birthdays and their personalities. We are moving out of a 2000 year 'Iron age' characterised by struggle and oppression and base instincts of power over others, and dense low vibrations – and now we have entered the 'Golden age' of enlightenment, love, spirituality, joy and higher vibrations.

The above explanation is related to astrology and astronomy which are both used in a prophetic way related to the unquestioned influences, over everything, that the stars (energy) and their relative positions in the Universe have. But the 'change' that's coming is also caused by many other factors on a Universal and Multiversal level and will effect far more of Creation than just Earth. However the changes to Earth are what mainly concerns us for now.

In preparation, it would seem, for this change, this 'Golden Age' Earth's vibrations *are* speeding up – getting higher. *'For thousands of years the Schumann Resonance or 'pulse' (heartbeat) of Earth has been 7.83 cycles per second, however, since 1980 this resonance has been slowly rising. Some scientists believe that it is rising faster than we can measure seeing as it is constantly rising while measuring'*. As you 'awaken' assuming you do 'wake-up' to the awesome possibilities of human life - far beyond your current dense and relatively low vibrational 3D life, your own vibrations also rise, to stay in harmony with Earth.

Perhaps you have heard about the biblical phenomenon known as Ascension? The idea behind this is that if you give your life to the worship of 'Jesus the *Saviour*' (only *you* can save yourself) and pray, and renounce sin, and all that, come 'Judgment Day' (whenever that is) you, your Soul, will rise to Heaven, you will 'ascend' and leave all the none believers and the rest of the plebs (non-Jesus freaks) behind to 'wither in the wilderness', or to face Armageddon, or whatever the nasty fate is that awaits the 'non-ascended'? Although not in the way just described, this 'prophecy' from the Bible, is not such a myth – it is just that the interpretation of it is not correct. The Ascension actually refers to the passing over to a higher vibrational, more spiritual, less dense, dimension due to the raising of the activity in your DNA from 33% to 40+%. And worshiping 'Jesus' and renouncing sin is symbolic of your 'awakening' from the current Archontic 3D world and seeing the 'light', that is, realising who and what you really are – limitless potential. And not some mind-controlled wage-slave labourer struggling through life just to serve the agenda of the ruling Elite. Hey, I like my life as it is thank you, I have what I need and a nice family and an OK job, why should I care about moving to a different dimension. I like it here.

That's all well and good I am happy for you in your blissful ignorance. However, just open your eyes a little, look around you, all the problems in the world, that apparently do not concern you at the moment, cannot simply be brushed under the carpet and they *will* affect you and your family eventually. If you are not a part of the evil Archontic Elite, your destiny, like that of everyone else, is ever more change for the worse, ever more dumbing down and enslavement.

Agenda 21 is *not* a fiction, or something that will happen in the way distant future, it is happening *now.* Your health *is* under attack, your life span *is* being severely limited, this simply cannot be denied, however much you might want to. Your freedoms are being eradicated and the world is rapidly falling into ever more chaos, and this will not stop – or get better - unless *you* do something about it yourself. Just because you are not effected too much now is not justification for denial, because you and your family certainly *will* be in a few years or less. If you are happy and content now, enjoy it as much as you can, because you won't be for much longer. Buy your health insurance – to (financially) take care of your inevitable future ill-health and trust your ('trained killer') doctor to help. Get on the latest fad diet, go running on your treadmill and be disappointed by the results (again!). Go shopping, enjoy profit inspired and created, and usually ridiculously naff, fashion. Go to 'therapy' and get a dose of common sense for an extortionate fee. Fill your house with (usually unneeded) possessions. Go out and discuss celebrities or sports over a beer. Participate in all the 'distractions' you can afford, to make your life/experience more enjoyable (bearable?) but, at the same time, try to realise how incredibly special and valuable your 'life' really is – to you and to others.

There is no way that everyone on the planet will 'awaken' – due to many reasons, ignorance being the chief one, and, unfortunately for the people who don't 'wake up' an ever shortening life, of ever deepening misery and ever more control over everything they do, is the *only* outcome while the Demon influenced ruling Elite are in charge.

Am I personally worried about things as they are? No, because I know that for me (which is why I am here on Earth at this particular time) things are going to be amazing in the future. I feel privileged to be living through this time of great change and to be a part of it. I feel I am in this world, but not a part of it. Of course I have to do all the things necessary to live. I have to play the 'game' for now and try to be as comfortable as I can, despite the problems finding food that is not tainted and toxic, and finding I am forever rolling my eyes at all the blatant lies and deception and corruption I now recognise every day. I try not to worry about anything, I try to keep as healthy as I can, mentally (despite my mercury fillings and previous fluoride poisoning) and physically. And I understand that any challenges I might face on a daily basis are all there to give me more experience, and to be used as stepping-stones towards my goal of 'ascension' to a life of love and peace and harmony (ah, and none GMO foods!)

If you do not know that a MacDonald's burger, or any other fast food outlet's burger, is poisoned (deliberately) and highly toxic to Human health (for reasons of profit, inducing long-term ill-health, and eventually towards the culling of people) you might enjoy the chemically synthetic taste of it and eat as many as you want. However if you know the truth, you may still eat them and to hell with your health, that is your choice. At least now you *have* a choice. On the strength of your knowledge you might (like me) never eat a burger again. Knowledge has given you a choice, before that you were just an unwitting dupe/victim. It is the same with everything I have been telling you here. This is now your knowledge, and now you have a choice – believe it and act upon it, or deny it and carry on as you are, to the eventual and *certain* detriment of your well-being. But, at least you are not an unwitting victim any longer. You may *choose* to remain a 'victim', but that is now a conscious decision (freewill) and not the result of simple (maybe blissful?) ignorance. And if you just do not believe me (I am only the messenger here) easy – do some research for yourself *before* you show your immaturity by simply decrying everything here, in your ego-driven ignorance.

I sincerely hope (for your sake) that you *are* feeling (subconsciously) the change in Earth's energy/vibrations, in, at least, some small ways – restlessness, a nagging 'knowing' that things are not quite right, occasional feelings of unexplained optimism, and also of unexplained dread. A perception of change in your life, an awareness of futility - a lack of meaning to your life, quite severe mood swings, poor sleep and occasional unexplained nausea and dizziness. These, amongst many others, are symptoms of the vibrational changes and if you have any of them it would suggest you are ready to 'awaken' to what life really is – far more expansive, spiritual, meaningful, exciting and interesting, than your current left-brained, programmed, 3D perception of reality.

"If we all did the things we are capable of, we would astound ourselves."

33

Good, Good, Good Vibrations...

The vibrational changes that *are* happening, *to* Earth and *on* Earth, have the potential to help you, or cause you, to alter or adjust many facets of your 'life experience'. Chief among these life-changing potentials are those to your whole well-being. Another advantage of 'waking up' and seeing the-wood-for-the-trees, of really understanding that life on Earth as a Human Being is far more extensive than being a programmed, evolved from a monkey, wage-slave (whether you are successful at that or not), is the inevitable improvement to your overall health.

Higher vibrations - as created by inner-calm, love, peace, joy, harmony, lack of fear and hate, and the realisation that you *are* being deceived, and lied to, and taken for a fool (and with that knowledge you can do something about it) will make a dramatic change in you.

Earlier I eluded to higher vibrations having the potential to change eating habits - (which is the major cause of *all* ill health). When you 'wake up' and tune into the higher vibrations that your 'awakening' will create, you will realise just how much you have been subconsciously programmed and controlled throughout your life by evil influences and you will rail against them.

You will begin to question just why are there so many (toxic) chemicals put into food – and not just merely accept it. Well, of course many are preservatives and put in to keep the food fresh. Not everyone has the opportunity, or can afford, to buy fresh fruit and vegetables everyday you know. And this is the point. Fruit and vegetables are free – provided by Mother Nature, the only food Humans need, grown in the earth. But of course they are not free (unless you grow your own – and who has time for doing that?). Fruit and vegetables are (over) priced at a premium, because of their known health benefits. What good are you to the ever more profit seeking Medical profession (industry) if you are healthy? The human body was not designed to, so it cannot, digest chemicals. All chemicals that are ingested are simply stored away in fat. Even most so-called health foods have chemicals in them, as preservatives, sweetners, enhancers etc. and these are all contributors to the build up of body fat.

Another reason for the transfer of wealth - through ever increasing taxes and and debt interest and (unjustified – or falsely justified) price increases for everything, is to prevent people from affording such 'luxuries' as fruit and vegetables. Sell 'em cheap chemically produced 'Pot Noodles' and burgers instead – it's 'food' in'it and tastes good...(?)

Ah, many chemicals in food are preservatives – better to have a few chemicals in you than bad and gone-off food. But, there are also many chemicals used as flavour enhancers and artificial colouring - how far have we, innately intelligent, Humans been programmed that we now buy and eat food according to its colour? (which we evidently do, otherwise why is the colour added?)

Aspertame is an artificial sweetener used extensively in diet sodas (diet Pepsi, diet Coke etc.) and sugar-free chewing gum – and many other foods. It is also one of the deadliest toxins known to man – and they put *this* in drinks and in food products and advertise them as 'healthy' options!? for the dullards and sheeple (you and me) to ingest and destroy our health - for their benefit! (in terms of profit - and power and control). I grew up drinking Diet Pepsi, the cool, healthy way to drink Cola. I shudder when I think how duped I was by the advertising (blatant lies) and how much of this heinous and poisonous product I consumed. Did it do you any harm? Heck, of course it did. I was a sportsman, I trained and kept fit and watched what I ate (doing the usual dumb thing - counting calories) and it was a constant struggle keeping a consistent weight. As soon as I stopped drinking Diet Pepsi (no other change) I could eat more food and still easily keep my weight lower. I also attribute Diet Pepsi to many other health disorders I used to suffer, such as being easily prone to injuries, tiredness, lowering eye sight power, even leading to later life arthritis.

Virtually all manufactured or processed food has chemical taste enhancers added to it, now what does that tell you? It should tell you that you are being programmed to eat food more according to (artificial) taste than nutrition. It is incredible to me that real lemon juice is used in the making of furniture polish and an artificial lemon flavour chemical is used in a Lemon Meringue pie! *You happy to be in a world like this?*

Even if it's nothing more than wanting to 'fight' back against the evil demonic-influenced food manufacturers who are systematically (deliberately) poisoning you, that motivates your change in diet (as it was for me at first) it is a start. But then as you start to 'de-program' yourself and raise your vibrations and realise what a wonderful thing your ever rejuvenating body really is and how much it has been abused and battered with chemicals, your taste buds will begin to go through a subtle change. You will begin to desire what is good for your body rather than what you simply and thoughtlessly crave. You will begin to look more carefully at labeling on food packaging and become a little more discerning about what you consume.

Your taste for sugar will gradually diminish when you realise the very serious harm it does to your body. Remember everything in creation is basically just a form of energy, vibrations, and food has vibrations. Processed and chemical tainted food has much lower vibrations than living foods, such as fruits and vegetables, and as your own vibrations get higher your desire for higher vibrating food will increase. Your thoughts for short-term gratification (hit of sugar) through cakes, cookies and candy (empty, useless and health damaging calories) will decrease and you will find yourself more inclined towards healthier options.

Stop and exercise some critical thinking again for a moment. Why do you think there are, and have been, so many different 'Diets' being promoted and sold? Of course everyone has different eating habits and cravings and different 'Diets' cater for these differences. But surely the *main* purpose of a 'Diet' is to help a person reduce their body weight (permanently) regardless of food preferences – and there are so many of them because they simply do not work in the long-term. Sure many people do lose weight in the short-term when they go on a 'Diet', but the weight drop is hardly ever sustained. 'Diets' are not designed to work – they are designed to be highly profitable. The *only* way an overweight person, addicted to modern processed foods, can lose weight and get back to a healthy body-weight ratio *permanently* is by a change of lifestyle and taste (taste buds).

Increasing your body vibrations and recognising and appreciating the higher vibrations that *true* knowledge will bring is the best 'Diet' – the *only* 'Diet', that will work to bring you back to your natural body weight – and sustain it. Of course this is much easier said than done I understand and even knowing that the 'food' (is it really food anyway? most of the time) you are eating is deliberately poisoned and designed (with chemical 'enhancers') to be addictive, does not make it any less difficult for people to give it up.

A trick I learned when I first started to change my eating habits and lifestyle, which was very effective for me, was to imagine that I had already just eaten the cookie (dipped in tea) that I craved, or the plate of fries, or the bowl of (laboratory produced) cereals and try to think how I felt. Was it really enough that my (distorted) taste-buds had been assuaged with a 'hit' of pleasurable (but pointless) taste, did I feel healthier and happier after my imaginary 'fix'? Would eating it really have added anything to my life? Of course the answer was no in all cases. Imagining I had just eaten and savoured the gratifying taste of a bag of crisps (chips) for example, which would have done *nothing* for me in terms of nourishment and health, and then actually eating an apple instead, which of course does have nourishment and health benefits, helped me greatly through the first few weeks of withdrawals and adjustment from processed food to natural, not in a packet, 'Whole foods'. I felt immediately healthier knowing I had just eaten something my body needed and not just what my (programmed) mind craved.

Many people advocate eating only raw foods as the only true way of totally cleansing and rejuvenating your body and curing yourself of all disease, and I would go along with that, to a degree. However that is an extreme life-style change, not only in diet, but also in social, and often professional, aspects of your life and I do not agree that finding and choosing food should become the be-all and end-all of your existence. A diet of natural whole foods, without a can or a box in your larder, will get you back to your natural weight quickly and greatly improve your health.

(Unfortunately) wheat, barley, rye and grains are *not* 'health' foods and eating them *will* have negative consequences to your health and body weight. That includes any type of bread – wholemeal, brown...whatever. There is enough information about this on the Internet, should you wish to research it further, without me adding to it – suffice to say giving up bread was my main priority - and biggest sacrifice. However we Humans are nothing if not resourceful and now I make my own healthy bread (very easy) from pre-soaked and dried desiccated coconut, buckwheat flour (which is not wheat) and tapioca starch. There are many healthy bread recipes on the Internet - google 'non wheat bread'.

Let your ever increasing energy vibrations, resulting from your 'awakening', guide you, through synchronicity and more discernment, to a better and more fulfilled life experience, and begin a detoxification of your body and your mind. Realise that, although (at the moment) you will be facing heavy odds against you, you *do* have more control over your thoughts and mind than the advertisers and food manufactures give you credit for – and, like the controlled, propaganda 'News', take with a pinch of salt any, and all, advertising for 'healthier' food options - or *any* ''health foods' that have been manufactured. Hit back at the evil money (power and control) influenced people and corporations who are using you simply as a docile, easily manipulated, dumb cash-cow. Boycott processed foods. Don't keep paying these evil people (and that's exactly what the people at the top of all major food corporations are) to poison you and attack and undermine your health.

It is often difficult to avoid all foods that are less than healthy, but with a balanced diet and everything in moderation your health and weight will improve. And eventually, if you 'listen', your body vibrations will start telling you what it needs, rather than what your mind wants.

A few years ago a book called "The Secret", which was a self-help book explaining how to manifest changes in one's life, was very popular. There are many other such books as well that go into great detail of how to get what you want from life. Many people have bought these books to learn the 'Secret' knowledge of how to improve the quality of their lives and found that repeitive positive affirmations and visualizations are the key to success. However the 'secret' behind the 'secret' (that many of these books miss) as I have already explained, is that *everything* in existence is energy/ vibrations. Einstein said *"Everything is energy and that's all there is to it. Match the frequency of the reality you want and you cannot help but get that reality. It can be no other way. This is not philosophy. This is physics."*

Although the concept of matching one's frequency (vibrations) to the 'reality' you want sounds quite daunting it actually isn't. With an 'awakening' (realising that there is so much more to this world, and your life than you think) your energy vibrations will naturally get higher - as you lose the fear and stress and anger that ignorance has caused. When you can accept that you are much more than a programmed 'wage-slave' for the ruling cabal, that you are all powerful, an omnipotent Being, life-changing manifestations can occur much more easily. *The amount of time it takes you to get from where you are to where you want to be, is only the amount of time it takes to change the Vibration within you.* 'Wake-up' to what is going on around you, thereby raising your vibrations - and synchronicity will more easily provide 'pathways' for you to follow to vastly improve the quality of your life. It cannot fail, as Einstein said – "there can be no other way".

"To live is the rarest thing in the world. Most people just exist."

34

Conclusion

As you have discovered throughout these past pages – 'we' are certainly a *LOT* more than you realised (or more accurately – than you *remembered*). We, as Humans, are in essence (or would have been, but for the parasitic Demons) Beings of all possibility. We should have (and *will* have, someday) no limitations on what we can perceive as possible. We are eternal Spirits/Souls/Consciousness on a never-ending journey of discovery through the experiences in different 'body/computer vehicles' in different times and on different worlds.

I have hardly scratched the surface here of the knowledge of, shall we call it 'Quantum Reality', for the want of a better rubric? I have personally studied thousands of hours, researching and finding, often with amazing synchronicity, different parts of this labyrinthine jigsaw that we call 'life on Earth'. There are many hundreds of thousands of people, possibly, by now, millions of people who are 'awakening' as the result of the afore mentioned changes in vibrations of Mother Earth. All these people – every one of them are now contributing to the collective knowledge of the 'Ocean' - the Vibrational Energy information/knowledge field which is an intrinsic part of all Creation. This knowledge (*all* the knowledge of *everything*) is accessible by everyone to a lesser or greater degree, depending on their perceptive awareness and mind-set. 'Heart knowledge', intuition, 'remembering', are all manifestations of accessing this knowledge. Spirituality, psychic, gnostic, 'channelling', meditation, DMT mind expansion, dream and hypnosis are all methods of gaining this knowledge, plus, in many cases, direct communications with Higher Beings.

You have arrived here after being bombarded with 'belief system' busting information and knowledge and your head is now spinning with contradictory thoughts and feelings. You know, inwardly, innately, that many of the things I have discussed, are possible, even probable. But the nagging doubts, fostered by your educational programming and up-bringing and left-brained logic, and by your 3D life experiences, remain. Take this chance to break free of these doubts and your reservations. Even if half, or more, of what I have postulated is an antipathy to you, or even if it is untrue (in *your opinion of* reality) there is still enough obvious and self-evident knowledge (surely) to give you pause for mentation. Do *not* dismiss *anything* out-of-hand, without due consideration and critical thought – and your *own* research beyond the mainstream paid for, tightly controlled and deliberately distorted knowledge.

Who am I?

Who are *we*? We are far from the person we think we are. We are not John Smith the butcher, or Shirley Jones the hairdresser, or Geoff Barraclough the teacher. We are infinite and eternal 'Consciousness', Spirit, Souls, simply having an 'experience' on this planet at this time, as a butcher or hairdresser or teacher, as part of our perpetual cosmic journey to ever higher enlightened dimensions. Whoa, sounds great! Yes, it does and be happy because that really *is* how it is.

Let's think (carefully) for a minute...How can 'life' with the awesome beauty and the complexity of the human computer/body vehicle and spirit, and a benign God/Creator/Energy (within everyone) be so unfair? On the one hand - the person going through life severely handicapped. The child whose 'life' is cut short by a tragic 'accident'. The young man whose life is wasted killing, and then being killed, in a senseless war. The baby who is a sacrificial victim of the Queen's or the Pope's Satanic rituals. The people suffering untold hardships in poverty just trying to survive for a few more days. The beggar on the dirty streets of an over-crowded city with nothing to look forward to except their next meagre meal.

On the other hand - the gifted and talented virtuoso. The person 'sailing' through life with few real challenges. The 'rich' (in monetary terms) and famous. The professional footballer, actor, or rock star, idolised by millions. Wow! What a lottery your birth is! *Surely* though there must be more to it than that? There is. This 'life' you are living now is just one of an infinite number of lives, just an 'experience' for your Consciousness/Spirit/Soul to learn and grow from. There is just no conceivable way that a God/Creator/Source/Energy, or nature, whatever we call it, would or could make choices about what type of life you are going to have, or no life at all (aborted or stillborn foetus) in a one-off deal. Well, you're going to suffer disability all your (only) life... you're going to be 'killed' at an early age...and you're going to be everything you can dream about. Not even the most sceptic and left-brain thinker would just accept that with little more than a shrug and a 'ce est la vie'. Surely, you must believe that the life of a beautiful and Gordian Human Being is more than just a lucky, or unlucky, turn-of-the-cards? Please, if nothing else, understand that we are *not just* cosmic accidents, the natural results of pure luck (bad or good) that mainstream science are desperate to have you believe.

We are all the off-spring of one race of Extra Terrestrials or another. Our DNA is under developed, deliberately suppressed, but we all have the potential, given the chance, and it *is* coming, to increase our DNA activity and to be Higher Beings, like our ancestors - if we take it.

What am I?

What are *we*? We are holographic projections in a holographic 'game'. We each have a 'Higher self' in control of our 'game' (life). We are energetic, computer-like vehicles for our Consciousness, our eternal Souls, to enable us to experience and react with the dense vibrational 3D reality that we perceive and call 'life' on this Planet. Think again about the awesome complexity of the human body and the human mind, and then think about, the base occurrences we are endlessly projected with, that cause fear, depression, illness, disease, frustration, anger, stress, anxiety, and all the rest of the low vibrational states. We have to rise above these situations that are enforced upon us and make the most of our God/Creator/Source given abilities for enlightenment and love and joy. Escape the 'trap' of 3D thinking and realise that *anything* is possible. This particular 'experience' on this particular planet, at this particular time is *not* just a fortuity of your birth, it is meant to be. Your experience ('life') here on Earth *is* for a reason. Whatever limitations you imbue yourself with (due to your programmed belief systems) you are, we all are, in fact – as David Icke says... "All Possibility - All that ever has been and All that ever will be!" We all have limitless potential.

Escape (as we *will,* eventually) from the Archontic Demon influences and personal time travel, telepathy, and spiritual 'astral' travel, and a Utopian existence will be possible, and, in fact, *normal* experiences for everyone. This is how it was meant to be and you are here, now to help facilitate this in some way, even if you have no idea how yet. No life is wasted, no matter how mundane or insignificant it may seem to be. Your 'Higher self' Consciousness/Spirit/Soul will guide you to experiences, good and bad, that will allow for learning and 'education' and preparation for your next 'life' on the next part of your Spirit's endless astral travels, wherever that may be.

Why am I here?

Why are we here? We are here as a part of our eternal cosmic journey through the Dimensions. We are here on Planet Earth right now, in the lowly and dense third dimension, to gain an 'experience', and to possibly help towards moving humanity away from the insidious Archontic/Satanic control. If you 'awaken' - that is realise and accept that 'life' is much more than you thought it was, your body/spirit energy vibrations will get higher and you will remain in tune and in harmony with Earth's increasing vibrations. This will result in your eventual 'ascension' to the next less dense and more spiritual dimension. Maybe it is your purpose to help others, family and friends, to see the 'light'. Or maybe it is your purpose to stay closed-minded and 'happy' with your lot, and remain for the rest of your life/experience in 3D as a wage-slave and a mind-controlled 'victim' – tempted to say moron, but that would be unfair. If this is the case, do not worry your life will still be worthwhile (though far less fulfilling) as a 'learning experience' for your Soul.

After all the research and 'dot connecting' that I have been doing during the past three years and the innate and heart knowledge I have been *'remembering'*, and my connection to the cosmic knowledge field. I am beginning to figure out why I personally am here at this point in time. In case you are interested...It all started for me when aimlessly surfing Youtube I came across some guy who had a video presentation that lasted for eight hours! It was David Icke's live solo presentation about the Perception of Reality on a stage in a theatre in London. I started to watch it thinking it was bound to put me to sleep in a few minutes, how can anyone bleat on for eight hours? After five minutes I was 'hooked' and I stayed up all night and watched it from start to finish – and then put it on again. Icke was saying some of the most outrageous things I had ever heard, but somehow I just knew what he was saying was right. It was as if I already *knew* everything he was talking about and he was just reminding me – a very strange experience. I analysed my life and realised looking back that I was, for some reason, being protected from the majority of the Archontic influences. I was never left-brained, nor enticed by money or possessions and I questioned everything I was told, particularly at 'Sunday School' (Religious 'education' as it was then). I knew the history I was being taught at school was not quite right, it was all too glib – but at that time I didn't know how or why. I could go on here for pages, but enough to say I have been 'protected' all my life, through good and bad experiences, obviously for a purpose.

Possibly that purpose is you reading this thesis. If I help to 'awaken' just one person, who has an influence on others, maybe that is why I am here. I know I am here to help, in some way, to get the evolution of mankind back on track. Perhaps I am even a Pleiadian 'light worker' – not such a fanciful concept considering that we are *all* the 'relatives' of different races of Extra-Terrestrials. Perhaps I am here to be laughed at and ridiculed for my ludicrous and idiotic notions (by you?) if that is the case I am happy to be in excellent company, with the greatest *free* thinkers on the planet.

**Never regret.
If it's good, it's wonderful.
If it's bad, it's experience.**

35

Final Words

Unless you were already 'awake' (God/Creator/Source bless you for your contribution to the higher vibrations of the world) you have just read probably the most challenging (to your belief system) text of your life. You are now faced with the choice of deciding what you make of it all.

Perhaps your mind tells you that it's OK, you have just read a work of total fiction, so nothing to even think about. I assure you *none* of this thesis is in any way a figment of my apparently over-active imagination – heck, I just couldn't make any of this up even if I tried. *Everything* I have 'talked' about is <u>verifiable and proven</u> with fact and/or empirical evidence. *Everything* I have mentioned you can (if you want, or can be bothered to) research yourself to find the source of the knowledge I am passing on here.

Perhaps, regardless of the factual and provable information here, your reaction is still denial – you don't *want* to know this truth, you like your 'world' and life as it is (was) and want no further complications' in it. Unfortunately you will not be able to simply forget all of this, parts of the knowledge you have gained here *will* affect you in subtle ways in the future, whether you like it or not.

Already changes in your perceptions are taking place despite your left-brain programmed, protesting denials.

Perhaps you can accept *some* of the things cited here, but are struggling to digest others. I would say this, if you accept even a single notion in this book then you are, at least, 'awakening' a little – however I would fail to understand how you can regard parts of this equally researched document as the truth and other parts you can't. I think that would surely prove to you that it is your 'programmed' and mind-controlled belief system that is 'kicking in' and causing your doubts. I know I come from a stand point of many thousands of hours of research but virtually everything I purport here is almost obviously self-evident, if you *look* and think *critically* about it.

I can only suggest that you 'open your eyes' to what is going on in your own little 'reality'. Do *you* think everything in the garden is rosy in the world? Can you not recognise blatant corruption when you see it? Do you think it's just the way of things (luck of the draw) that a billionaire in a $5,000.00 suit in a Rolls Royce drives past beggars on the streets with nothing? Do you think it is natural that the world is in constant war, apparently all caused by the (mythical) 'terrorist' threat? Have you ever seen a 'terrorist' (or heard of one) apart from on the made-up mainstream news, who has ever tried to hi-jack a plane with a 100ml tube of tooth paste? (as opposed to a 20ml one that you *are* allowed to take on a plane). Don't you see (like I do) all the little old ladies being treated as potential 'terrorists' at the airport security checks and like everyone else having to remove their shoes? (despite going through the health damaging, radiating, body scanners). Are they looking for a concealed hat-pin, with which the old dear is going to attack a flight steward? It is a total joke. Even the 'security' personnel have no idea really what they are looking for in a pair of shoes. Of course you just accept all this without any thought as, well that's just the way it is. Which is exactly the point. Have you ever drank from your (transparent) water bottle in front of the airport 'security' people, proving that the liquid inside is not a toxic substance or acid with which I can only imagine you are going to burn the carpet in the plane until it turns round and takes you to...where – Iran? (Life is much better and freer there than America, so good choice) and they still take it off you. You can buy more water inside mate – yeah, at three or four times the normal price. Ooooh I don't mind – better than having those 'terrorist' chappies threatening the plane with dodgy water. I could go on and on about the ludicrous farce that is air travel nowadays – full 'naked' body scanners, whatever they call them, that gives you an equivalent dose of 20 years of natural radiation in one go, and no doubt some of the 'security' staff a cheap thrill, every time you go through one, but you get my point? Hmm, I wonder how many paedophiles or perverts are applying for jobs in 'security' at airports?

It is no accident that you have read this – it is synchronicity, one thing leading to another to another that brought you here, for a reason, a purpose. You may have no clue yet what that purpose is, but it will manifest itself in small - or even significant ways, in your future. As I have said this knowledge is now in your brain, whether it is welcome or not, it can be denied, but it cannot be unread now.

Perhaps all of this has struck a chord with you – and like me, you just knew somehow, that something was wrong with life as it is, and you may go on to further develop your knowledge with your own research. Good for you and welcome to the wonderful...? Perhaps not yet, but much better, world of the 'awoken'. Every-day life will, has to, go on, but for you things will never quite be the same. Your 'vibrations' will be higher, you will have less stress and anxiety, and this will create less low vibrational 'food' for the Archons - which will help towards their demise (your contribution towards a better future for everyone). What can you be stressed about when you know that this life is only a 'game', an experience to learn from and you will be back (here or somewhere else) whatever happens.

Perhaps, like me you, will do more research into the (toxic) food you eat and, to the immense benefit of your future health, weight and longevity, and your families health, avoid as much of it as you can. You will look at other people, not with distaste at their greed, or rudeness, or arrogance, or ignorance, but with sympathy for their obvious controlled and limited 3D mind-set – as yours, and mine, *used* to be.

Whatever happens in your life, stay positive. Life is just a mirror of your thoughts and actions. If something happens in your life that you don't like – consider this brilliant insight by David Icke...

'Think about what you don't like as looking at the reflection of yourself in a stream. You can throw rocks into the water, until your reflection disappears, you can jump in the stream and splash and thrash about and your reflection will vanish but when you stop doing all these things, it will still be there reflecting back at you. Nothing will have changed. If something happens that you don't like change the *cause* of the problem, not the symptoms of it'. Expect the worse and invariably the worse will happen. Expect the best and 'aim' for it and it *will* happen. Life may throw some challenges at you along the way, but these challenges are *meant* to occur, they are deliberate and the solutions to them will lead you ever closer to what it is you want from your 'life' (from your Earthly *'experience'*).

Most people want to manifest more money into their lives, but this is a totally false precept – the thought that it is money that can change your life for the better. It is not money, or the things it can buy, that will make the difference, but more your appreciation of it related to your circumstances. Set yourself a more lofty goal to aim for; a more comfortable life, a life with less stress, a life with a holiday home to relax at, a life with more time for yourself, a life in a different location, a life with better health, a life with more labour saving tools, a life with a more fulfilling occupation, a free from worry retirement etc. The finances you will require (until such time as money is a thing of the dark and demonic past) will come to you in various and unexpected ways. Wishing to win the lottery, just for the money (power and control) to decide later what you want to do with it will not get you far. Although, of course, some people *do* win the lottery - but these people are often faced with other challenges in their lives as a result of the win. Remember, whatever happens to you, nothing in life (the 'game') is just luck (good or bad) it is all for a reason, an 'experience', a part of the never ending learning journey of your Consciousness.

Geoffrey Barraclough

As I have already mentioned it really is no accident or mere random chance that you have just read this, the increasing vibrations of Earth, and subsequently your own higher energy vibrations, have determined it. It is synchronism, a pre-destined occurrence, and from now on ever more synchronicity will lead you to ever more information such as this. You will search on Youtube for natural cures for a cold or flu or a cough, to avoid chemical drugs and their side-effects, and you will see, become more aware of, many other informational presentations that will have a positive effect on your health and spirituality. Your addiction to health-destroying sugar and other toxic foods will gradually diminish as you become ever more 'enlightened' about your body and your reason for being. You will start to alter your view of the world and of your place in it. Thoughts of just another cigarette, or just another beer, or cheese burger or doughnut won't do me any harm - "ah, we all have to 'go' sometime and everyone gets fat as they get older"...will begin to fade as you realise you are not here on this planet at this time just to pass time struggling and being controlled, and duped, and dumbed down, and easily gratified, and poisoned, before severe ill health leads to the early demise of your body/vehicle. Your time here is incredibly valuable and not just to you, but to everyone else too. It is a learning experience and the more you learn and experience and the more you can add to the cosmic 'knowledge matrix' (for everyone's benefit) this time around will make it so much better for when you come back.

They say there is nothing more certain than death and taxes in this life, of course this is just a jest, a diversion, a simplistic untruth to keep you in your place. There is no death, (of your Soul/Consciousness), and taxes are actually *legally* optional, voluntary. However there *is* nothing more certain than change. Earth and the Universe (multiverse) *is* changing, dramatically, and life is evolving rapidly now – the current Demonic control system cannot be sustained in higher energy vibrations.

My final, final words are these...

Try to make the most of your time here, gain as much 'true' knowledge and meaningful experience as you can, in preparation for the next stage of your wonderful cosmic journey to enlightenment.

I sincerely thank you, and appreciate your effort, for getting to the end of this thesis. I have no need to hope that, by reading this, things will get better for you – because I *KNOW* they will.

Life is based on perception.
Perception is based on opinion.
Opinion is based on thought.
Thought comes from mind.
Change your mind...
Change your life!

36

Acknowledgements

Many brilliant people have each contributed to my knowledge, through their websites, Youtube presentations, and physical and digital books and articles. I am massively indebted to all of them for my 'awakening' and opening my potential to evolve into a higher Dimensional Being. Of course this book could never have been written without the knowledge and inputs of these people - some of the best researchers, authors, presenters, 'whistle-blowers', 'channellers' and enlightened minds on the planet. I am grateful to each of them for adding their specialist areas of expertise to my overall understanding of 'Quantum Reality'.

I have not referenced *all* my information with specific quotes, documents, essay titles or websites for several reasons. One being the amount of space I would need to do so – the list of references would be longer than the work itself. Another reason is that there are, of course, so many differing views on so many of the contentious subjects I have covered that I would have to reference many different sources for each one, in the quest to be fair and objective. I do not know how interested the average reader would be in following a reference link for *every* bit of information I have presented. So rather, I have suggested some specific

Youtube and Goggle searches and recommended books, where relevant.

Also I have included here the names of a few of the top researchers and 'whistle-blowers in this field....

You can copy and paste (digital copy), or copy down each name (physical copy) and with a 'Google' search, or search on Youtube, you will be taken to a world of astonishing knowledge and cognition you never knew existed.

David Icke, Alfred Lemont Webre, Michael Tellinger, Lee Caroll/Kryon, Santos Bonacci, James Gilliland, Greg Braden, Richard D Hall, Judy Wood, Graham Hancock, Ken O'Keefe, Mike King, Simon Parkes, Michael Talbot, Lloyd Pye, Alex Jones, Alex Collier, Cathy O'Brian, Kerry Cassidy, Jorden Maxwell, Delores Cannon, Kate of Gaia, Teal Scott, Bill Ryan, Peter Kling, Lauren Moret, David Irving, Laura Magdalene Eisenhower, Andrew Basiago, Mary Rodwell, Peter Slattery, Zecharia Sitchin, Richard Dolen, Ken Rohla, Frank Chester, Robert Stanley, Jack Pruett, Timothy Good, Michael Salla, James Bartley, Susan Lindauer, Neil Sanders, Leonardo da Vinci

You can also visit my website; **http://awakening4u2. homestead.com** where there are direct links to all these people's websites, blogs or Youtube presentations.

If you don't think – then you shouldn't talk!

37

A Personal Perspective

I want to thank you again for sticking with me and ploughing your way through this book, despite the probable and arduous challenges you faced to your belief system.

Although this publication obviously reflects my *own* personal understanding and interpretation of all the knowledge I have accumulated over the years, I believe it to be 'in the ball park', at least, of the true version of reality. There are, of course a vast number of different interpretations and hypothesis' on this subject and I still have much to learn. Some finer points of my postulations may contain errors I will have to correct as I continue to compile knowledge. However the salient points are generally agreed upon by most researchers in this field. I certainly do not simply believe everything, or, in fact, *anything* I am told, without due consideration, critical thinking, real evidence and thorough research. I have heard it said many times that the reason many people do not accept 'Conspiracy theory' is that there are so many 'theorists' with different viewpoints and contrary information. And I have some sympathy with this argument, but, whether genuine or not, whether misinformed or not, whether pure in intent, or not, these people who hold an alternative view of reality, should, at the very least stimulate your curiosity and awaken you from your automaton-like dependence on the corrupt and tightly controlled (surely you can see it?) so often fake, mainstream media for your knowledge. The wonderful thing about Youtube for alternate information is the ease of access and the sheer amount of it. Also if 'they', the CIA and other intelligence agencies in the pocket of the ruling Elite, want to suppress and remove a particular video and they do, regularly, it is an easy task for whose ever video it is to get it up-loaded again.

The man who reads nothing at all is better educated then the man who reads nothing but newspapers.

(Thomas Jefferson)

Over the next few pages, if you are interested, I would like to further my discussion with a personal perspective of my own 'experience' of life.

The first thing to mention is I have always had a disdain for wealth and possessions. Money, other than to have enough for a reasonably comfortable 'journey' through my 'game' (life) has never been of any interest to me. As I mentioned I seem to have been 'protected' if I can call it that, from the base Archontic/Demonic emotions associated with its accumulation. I do not however hold any derogation for those who genuinely want to 'better' themselves and think the accretion of money is the way to do this. I do feel strongly about the attainment of money becoming the be-all-and-end-all of existence though if the process of getting it results in damage of any kind to fellow Human Beings. Which is all too often the case. In my opinion a doctor, for example, who knows full well the implications to a person's health of the drugs he is prescribing for them, so that he can profit towards affording a bigger house (or whatever) is the lowest of the low and is truly Demonic.

An interesting point here is; do we simply blame the influence of the Demons for all misdemeanour's and crime in the world? Of course this has massive implications and begs the question should I *hate* the doctor who pushes deadly drugs simply for profit, or the UK Queen for murdering babies and young children in Satanic rituals, or the ruling Cabal for their continuous evil genocide of the Human race? Well, apart from hate being a totally inutile emotion that I am not (thankfully) prone to, it is difficult, knowing what I do, to *not* have a degree of sympathy towards these people and *all* people who perpetrate crime of any level against Humanity. Perhaps this is what the symbolism of Jesus is all about. Forgiveness of a psychopathic lying, murdering scum bag - Bill Gates for example, that the mythical (mythical in the biblical interpretation) but emblematic/angelic 'Jesus' preached is just impossible surely...unless 'he' knew (which, of course hypothetically 'he' did) that these people were, and are, effected by forces, often, beyond their control. And the saving/redemption of a Soul regardless of their past 'sins' is a blessed thing for all concerned. One Being less for Satan and his Demons to have control over. Think about the Bible... "Forgive those that trespass against us..." only take it much deeper. Forgive the demonic influenced people if they repent their sins. Evil-doers, no matter how depraved and extensive their crimes against humanity might be, can be saved. Their Souls, like everyone else's, are eternal and will go on to have other 'experiences' on this or other worlds. Their next experience could be more enlightened and loving, or they could be held to task for their actions and forced to stay in the lower dimensions (symbolic of Hell?) Remember people who have been murdered by Evil-doers have only had one of their 'experiences' terminated prematurely, they will have many others.

However, saying all that I do believe that Human Beings, despite our restricted and controlled evolution, have acquired a certain degree of innate knowledge about right and wrong (empathy) and many people are able to fight against their evil demonic influences, instead of merely giving in to them for gain or base gratification.

I have been fortunate in my life that I have no cause at all for regret – if I had to live my life again I would not change a single thing in it. Should 'ave, could 'ave, would 'ave, has never applied to me. I guess knowing that even the bad times were nothing more than 'learning experiences' helps in this. I have heard it said that everyone *should* have regrets, otherwise they are displaying an appalling lack of empathy. I understand this. There is probably not one person alive who has not said the odd hurtful thing, in temper, or inflicted an injurious deed upon others, in reaction, or retaliation, or anger. Of course I am guilty of this as well and yes I would call it highly regrettable, but I am fortunate not to have done it enough to cause me such serious regret that I would wish I could change my life because of it.

Also I have been spared throughout my life of many of the low vibrational and dense emotions, such as depression, which my mother suffered horrendously from, and fear and jealousy. Perhaps I should own up to a little envy of fellow 'true-reality researchers' (for want of a better description) who have had out-of-body experiences, enlightening spiritual experiences, near-death experiences, or even direct contact with Higher Beings. However, although not having the benefit of these types of 'higher' 'education' I have been blessed with, at times, an unimaginable and freakish *innate* knowledge that has allowed me to develop my knowing in the way I have. It would appear that I am benefiting, subconsciously, from experiences I have had in past lives.

This particular life I am having now did not endow me with any really spectacular talents in the way of gaining any renown. However, I have sufficient natural ability to be just good enough to enable me to relish a moderately high standard of achievement in most things I do. I played to a reasonable amateur standard in many sports, high enough to enable me to successfully train as a PE teacher and I formed a personal mantra – there are only two ways of doing *anything*, your best – or not at all, which I live by. I have also developed my gift for art by following my attitude of accepting only the very best I can do at the time. I have always been a right-brain thinker. Mathematics, logic, group-think, the need to conform, were always a struggle for me. I gained 'educational' qualifications and a B Ed degree simply by following my self-imposed attitude of only doing my best, in whatever I did, even if it was of no real interest to me. Self-achievement has always been a defining factor in my life. I love being innovative, problem solving is my passion, thinking outside-the-box my modus operandi, and exploring all possibilities with an open-mind is my habitual approach to anything. Studying, the accumulation of knowledge (*real* knowledge) is what I live for - I guess, in preparation for the next stage of my cosmic journey.

The subject matter I am currently exploring – I call it 'Quantum Reality' for want of a better title has ticked all the boxes for my fulfillment in this game of life I am currently 'playing'. It is far more than a hobby or even an unpaid job. It is what I came back to this Earth at this time for. I hope, above all else, the writing of this work will convey to the reader, even just a little of the incredible sense of freedom and well-being that *true* knowledge can bring.

The vibrations of Earth *are* changing, getting higher and, whether you want to be a part of it (the great change) or not, you *will* be effected one way or another in time. It is unavoidable, however deeply your own (self-limiting) beliefs are entrenched. Why not just *try* to open your mind to more possibilities than your current restricted perception allows you to imagine? It will not ultimately cause any harm to your 'life' or your ego. Try opening up your 'box' of limited perception, just a little and see some of the alternatives to the shite and bleakness of the deeply restricted 3D world you inhabit. Do it quietly without fuss, just privately research a few Youtube video documentaries and presentations from the 'alternate media' (*NOT* "conspiracy theories" as you might *want* to believe they all are). Test-the-waters for yourself, before responding with "you're crazy" whenever someone tells you something that goes against your intractable 'grain'. Try searching **"Natural Cancer Cures"** on Youtube. It will take you a few minutes. Not only could doing this gain you invaluable and true knowledge, it could save your life or the lives of friends and family, as you learn the indisputable truth of the suppression of the natural cures for this deliberately exacerbated 'disease' and what you can do to avoid getting it or how to cure it yourself. Then search and watch **"Dr. Burzynski Cancer Cures"** also on Youtube. Once you have seen the disgusting beyond words, behaviour of the people responsible for putting profits before people in this case, you will seriously *have* to think - if some people are capable of doing this (they *are* evidently) then what else are they capable of – and why...? And then the door to 'wakefulness' will be ajar for you – and welcome!

Of course I had no idea about any alternative reality as I was growing up, like most people, life for me was just what it seemed to be, normal, ordinary and full of good and bad experiences, the good outweighing the bad for the most part. I do however remember obsessing about what comes after death – I somehow knew that there must be something more than just a one-time deal at life. I also remember from an early age I had dreams, often quite vivid, about travelling in space and visiting new worlds and planets and seeing the Universe as a playground. This was in the days before TV Space 'fiction' (fact) programs, so I had no idea where these dreams came from and just ignored them. I used to do lots of doodles in my school books involving planets and stars and little green men! At the time they meant nothing – just idle hands and a disinterested (in the lesson) mind. It is only now looking back in hindsight that I can see and understand the significance of these things. I was clearly recalling things from my past lives. I cannot think of any other explanation. What is the explanation, other than recall, for me being able to readily accept all the new information I have been exposed to over the past few years? – The very information many of you are struggling here to believe is anything more than delusional fantasy. Looking back at my life from the stand point I am at now, is very interesting, and I see so many seemingly meaningless or random, at the time, thoughts, actions and events, as now being very significant in shaping who I have become. Of course this happens to everyone, but not everyone is as comfortable as I am in knowing and acknowledging the true nature of reality - mores the pity, as far as the state of the world is concerned.

I truly believe, after all the research I have done – and am still doing, that, within my life-time (I am 61 years old – in 2015) the world in which we live will have undergone an extraordinary change. For those who 'want' it (those who *are able* to change their mind-controlled dogma) planet Earth will be a less dense fourth or fifth dimension paradise. You can be confident that your children will live a wonderful 'life'...they are here to ensure it happens. Unfortunately we have to survive the next few years, which are going to be pretty rough, as the Demons desperately fight a losing 'battle' against higher vibrations and enlightenment and who will, through their hybrid/human puppets, unleash further unspeakable horror and evil onto mankind. More HARRP created earthquakes and devastation around the globe (like Napal), more 'terrorist' attacks and shootings, more blatant lies and propaganda in the media (to control and shape public group-think) in an increasingly desperate effort to keep control of the masses. But, even if you don't survive, or you take absolutely no heed of this knowledge I am passing on to you, and you simply passively accept and wait for your inevitable ill-health and the premature demise of your body, while sticking to your limiting perception that I, and everyone like me, must be just wrong - imbecilic cranks! Your life will not be wasted, your Soul/Spirit/Consciousness will learn the 'truth' eventually, however many 'life experiences' it takes.

No one can fully predict the future – not even Higher Beings, nor will time-travel into the future (which is possible now - research *Andrew Basiago and Project Pegasus*) reveal the definitive version of the future. This is because, like life itself, the future is full of limitless potentials and possibilities. Small, even seemingly insignificant things like a few extra people 'awakening' and increasing the vibrations of the Cosmic Matrix/'Ocean' all around us, can affect the future in many different ways. Every event that happens (or is manufactured) and the response to it, has a negative or positive effect on the 'time-line' that we will experience. There are an infinite number of 'time-lines' (potentials) that we could travel and indeed not all people will travel the same time-line. However, due to all the changes I have been describing here (passing on information from highly intelligent, open-minded experts and specialists) it seems that Earth has moved onto a very positive time-line and the future...eventually, is bright! Full of Light.

Demonic Evil has had its day – the natural being of a Human Being is Love, and love will eventually triumph over evil. Face the challenges in your life/experience knowing that if you have the right mind-set you cannot lose, whatever happens...

EACH NEW DAY IS ANOTHER CHANCE TO CHANGE YOUR LIFE...

This thesis – as I have mentioned, barely goes beneath the surface of the humongous depth of the 'Rabbit Hole' that is 'life'. It is simply a basic starting point to discovering the virtually unlimited *knowledge* that makes up our existence as Human Beings. Of course there are no definitive answers to many questions about 'life'. The complexity of our being is such that there can only ever be conjecture and opinion regarding some aspects of the wider view of reality. This is because reality is simply what each person believes it to be. However the information I have cited here is based on provable fact, wherever possible - and on the widely accepted opinion of independent researchers and free thinkers, and of channeled information from Higher Beings, when absolute 'scientific' proof or evidence is not available.

But, what is *'scientific'* proof? The 'proof' required by many people before they can or will believe something? 'Scientific' proof is a concept of 3D thinking and of a limited perception of what is possible, brought about by a false and deliberately limiting education. Three dimensional science is only useful in the 3D world of dense vibration 'physicality' and five sense conceptualisation. It is also a highly controlled and very limiting construct, reducing the dissemination of known knowledge to a very restricted trickle. Science, as taught and publicly accepted, is little more than a tool of control - and certainly should not be the basis of your belief system.

Simply open your closed (controlled) mind and think critically and *independently* – become a *FREE THINKER* and so much more real knowledge will begin to flow to you...

WE'RE ALL IN THE SAME GAME JUST AT DIFFERENT LEVELS

PERCEPTION DECEPTION
By David Icke

www.davidicke.com

The greatest expose of Human life and reality ever written...

Critical Thinking - is the answer to the question...

An anthropologist proposed a game to children of an African Tribe. He put a basket of fruit near a tree and told the kids that the first one to reach the fruit would win them all. When he told them all to run they all took each other's hand and ran together, then sat together enjoying the fruits. When asked why they ran like that, as one could have won all the fruit for himself, they said

"Ubuntu, how can one of us be happy if all the others are sad?"

UBUNTU is a philosophy of African Tribes that can be summed up as...
"I am because we are"